Learning about Social Issues through Scripts for Learners aged 11–16

Learning about Social Issues through Scripts for Learners aged 11–16 offers secondary drama teachers a new and exciting approach to exploring social issues with their students. Focusing on the issues that matter to young people, it includes a wide range of classroom and performance materials carefully tailored for differing abilities and ages.

The book is based around four original play scripts – exploring themes of antisocial behaviour, eating disorders, the effects of war on families, and riots – that have been tried, tested and proven to motivate and engage young people. As well as building performance skills, each script is accompanied by detailed schemes of work to help students explore what the issues mean to them and develop their problem solving and thinking skills. The book also includes cross references to pedagogical techniques and approaches, assessment for learning and 'learning to learn' strategies.

Written by an experienced author team, *Learning about Social Issues through Scripts for Learners aged 11–16* provides a 'one-stop shop' for teachers to explore relevant and stimulating themes and topics that will engage students in lively debate, promote empathy and produce creative dramatic responses.

John Rainer is Leader of the Academic Division of Arts, Humanities, Language and Inclusion and PGCE Drama Co-ordinator within the Faculty of Education at Manchester Metropolitan University, UK. He has over thirty years' experience as a secondary drama teacher, local authority Advisory Teacher, Lecturer, Consultant and Youth Theatre Director.

Kirsty Walters is a drama specialist with 14 years' experience as a teacher in primary and secondary schools. Kirsty is currently Head of Drama at Fred Longworth High School, UK. In her role as Lead Practitioner she is responsible for whole-school teaching, learning and initial teacher training. Her work has involved in-house and outreach training, and liaison with various institutions in an advisory capacity.

Learning about Social Issues through Scripts for Learners aged 11–16

Tried and tested projects for teachers

John Rainer and Kirsty Walters

Routledge
Taylor & Francis Group

LONDON AND NEW YORK

First published 2014
by Routledge
2 Park Square, Milton Park, Abingdon, Oxon OX14 4RN

and by Routledge
711 Third Avenue, New York, NY 10017

Routledge is an imprint of the Taylor & Francis Group, an informa business

British Library Cataloguing in Publication Data
A catalogue record for this book is available from the British Library

Library of Congress Cataloging in Publication Data
Rainer, John, 1956-
Learning about social issues through scripts for learners aged 11–16 : tried and
tested projects for teachers / John Rainer, Kirsty Walters.
    pages cm.
1. Drama in education—Great Britain.   2. Drama—Study and teaching
(Secondary)—Great Britain.   3. Social sciences—Study and teaching
(Secondary)—Great Britain.   I. Walters, Kirsty.   II. Title.
PN2078.G7R35 2014
372.660941—dc23

                                                        2013045037

ISBN: 978-0-415-70313-0 (hbk)
ISBN: 978-0-415-70315-4 (pbk)
ISBN: 978-1-315-77529-6 (ebk)

Typeset in Celeste
by Swales & Willis Ltd, Exeter, UK

Contents

Introduction

This book came about as an attempt to alleviate a persistent problem in a particular secondary school in the north west of England: how to engage and motivate reluctant students – particularly boys – in drama lessons, and encourage them to study the subject beyond Key Stage Three 11–14 years.

In some schools in the UK drama is largely perceived as a 'girls' subject', with few boys opting to study it at examination level. Reluctance to participate in drama on the part of some young male learners seems to relate to their cultural perceptions of the subject, and to widely held negative stereotypes around those who practise it. This raises some tricky issues for drama teachers, and cracking the cultural norms responsible for this set of understandings about the subject is clearly outside the possibilities and remit of a humble textbook. However, getting reluctant students into drama also seems to have something to do with the choices about lesson *content* made by teachers for drama lessons and workshops, and this at least is something that might be addressed through a straightforward practical intervention.

Thus, the social issues around which the teaching units are based – and the structured approaches to teaching drama which are explored in this book – are specifically chosen to appeal to a wide range of learners across Key Stages 3–4 (ages 11–16) and in particular, but not exclusively, to less-motivated or under-confident boys.

The book is based around four mixed-cast play scripts which explore issues that have engaged the learners with whom we have worked: eating disorders – from a male perspective, antisocial behaviour, the effects of war on soldiers and their families, and the UK riots of 2011. Each of the scripts was written to appeal to the widest range of learners, and they have been tested and refined in workshops and performances with young people over a number of years.

Each script can be approached as a straightforward template for performance – suitable for 'off-the-peg' examination pieces at GCSE or A/AS level, as school plays, open evening presentation pieces or youth theatre performances. In addition, linked to each of the scripts are detailed and well-trialled schemes of work, which take different pedagogical approaches dependent on the age and experience of the learners. This allows teachers to plot their own pathway through the materials to suit the needs of their students, and provides a single location within which scripts, related performance workshops and issue-focused units of work are all located. Cross references to pedagogical techniques and approaches, assessment for learning, thinking skills and 'learning how to learn' agendas are all signposted.

Teaching and learning strategies used in the workshops

Throughout the workshops we have integrated a range of teaching and learning strategies designed to encourage collaborative learning, the development of 'thinking skills' and reflections on learning. These strategies are integrated into the fabric of the workshops, and are listed below:

- *Learner's log*: A log of work completed each workshop to enable learners to chart their progress and set personal targets for achievements (see example on p. 34).
- *Think time*: Opportunities for learners to broaden their thinking and engage in discussion.
- *Learning buddies*: Learners are paired up with one another and become mentors who guide each other's learning, set each other targets and peer-assess.
- *Thinking hats*: Based on the ideas of Edward de Bono, learners are asked to consider an issue or issues arising in the drama from a particular perspective, which is denoted by the colour 'hat' they are metaphorically wearing:
  - ○ Red hat = Emotions that are evoked by the issue: ... *my gut reaction and intuition tells me* ...
  - ○ Yellow hat = A positive perspective on the issue: ... *this might work, because* ...
  - ○ Black hat = Negative aspects of the issue: ... *what's wrong with this plan is* ...
  - ○ Green hat = Solutions/alternatives, creative thinking: ... *another way of thinking about this is* ...
  - ○ White hat = Facts, information and analysis: ... *what do we know about this?*
  - ○ Blue hat = Organising, directing, chairing: ... *can we think about what's needed here?*

- *Mix, share, pair*: In which learners move through the space (mix), stand opposite a partner when the teacher says 'pair' and share their thoughts or information when the teacher says 'share'.

- *Relay hot seat*: Learners move, in turn, onto the 'hot-seat' where they are quizzed, in role, by the rest of the class.

- *WWW/EBI (What went well?/Even better if . . .)*: Structured questions posed to individual audience members to elicit peer feedback for performers.

- *Extended learning tasks*: Homework tasks used to develop knowledge and understanding of issues/topics explored in lessons.

Anti-social behaviour

Introduction and context

This unit of work tackles the issue of 'antisocial behaviour', exploring the consequences of such behaviour, and providing learners with opportunities to reflect on their own values and experiences.

The sequences of workshops found in this unit are based around the play *ASBO*, which was originally written for an all-male cast of GCSE learners studying for their practical examination. The play and the units of work that accompany it were created as a method of encouraging the interest and participation of boys without excluding the girls in the class.

Antisocial Behaviour Orders (ASBOs) were first introduced in the UK in 1998 by the then Labour government of Tony Blair in an attempt to tackle antisocial behaviour by restricting the culprits – often by the use of electronic 'tagging' – from particular areas or behaviours, such as drinking alcohol or being out after dark.

A number of high-profile cases in the media at the time highlighted what was seen to be a growing problem – groups of 'feral' young people causing havoc and destruction within housing estates and town centres. For a while the newspapers were full of stories of *ASBO kids*, perhaps neglecting to point out that a large proportion of those receiving the orders were themselves afflicted with drug or alcohol problems, learning disabilities or mental health problems.

As a solution to the problem, however, ASBOs proved controversial; some regarded them as ineffective and expensive, whilst others saw them as a means of criminalising and demonising an already vulnerable and neglected section of society.

In 2010, ASBOs were abolished by the then Home Secretary Theresa May, to be replaced with the *Criminal Behaviour Order* (or CRIMBOs as they were soon named).

ASBO – The play

A note from the playwright

This play was originally written for a group of Year 11 (15–16-year-old) male General Certificate of Secondary Education (GCSE) learners as stimulus for their Unit 3 Edexcel GCSE Drama examination. All of the boys in this group were regarded as rather 'challenging' and were struggling with issues such as behaviour and low self-esteem. At the initial time of writing, the topic of 'antisocial behaviour' appealed to all learners but seemed to motivate the boys in particular; they achieved high-grade passes, and, more importantly, found the experience both enjoyable and hugely rewarding. The script has been repeatedly used in my own school – and others – as a method of raising the achievement of boys (without excluding the girls!), challenging the thoughts and views of its young people, and provides a platform for discussion and dramatic exploration. Despite the fact that the play contains five characters, it can easily be adapted to involve more characters – extra gang members, male or female – or other residents. Although some roles are smaller than others, I have always found that results achieved have been excellent and the impact on all performers involved in the piece has been profound. It is very much an ensemble piece and all characters are on stage throughout. Some scenes are particularly challenging, such as Scene 6, which demands a fast pace and high energy to encapsulate the atmosphere of chaos, intimidation and aggression.

As stated previously, at the time of writing this piece, 'antisocial behaviour' was extremely topical in the UK – as were ASBOs – seen by the government at the time to be a possible solution to youth crime and disorder. The play was an excellent vehicle for highlighting the causes and consequences of this type of behaviour and it went on to be presented to learners during school assemblies and in allocated Personal Social and Health Education (PSHE) time. It presents some great opportunities for cross-curricular collaborative projects. The set is minimal (although there are artistic opportunities for set design, graffiti art, etc.) and music is optional (although there is an opportunity for learners to incorporate their own choice of music to enhance the performance or to create their own 'stomp'-style pieces, which could easily be integrated into the performance). From my experience at my own school, I have always found that the subject matter appeals to all learners across Key Stages 3 and 4 and is something which rears its head in the press time and time again. I believe that the play has the potential to be used for many years without losing its dramatic appeal and topicality. It can be re-invented and adapted over time.

KW

ASBO

Kirsty Walters

Cast

Mr Jones: A 62-year-old man living on the estate
Scar: Gang member (all are aged between 14 and 16 years and live on the estate)
Big Jay: Gang member
Gaz: Gang member
Little Gee: Gang member

Scene 1

Set made up of gutters, pipes, bins, litter, etc. We hear the sound of water dripping and occasional noises that you might hear at night time. This could be done as a soundscape using objects that you might find lying around in the street. The cast slowly appear like cats creeping out of alleyways.

Mr Jones: (*offstage*) From the gutters, the alleyways, the sewers, like rats, they appear, out for the night. Time to play. Time to take ownership. Time to mark their territory. On the streets, in the doorways, on street corners, filtering through the estates, they gather, they goad, they terrorise, they . . .

All: Smash!

Gang: Your town, our town,
Your street, our street,
Your life, our life,
Watch your back!

Your night, our night,
Your time, our time,
Your estate, our estate,
What you looking at?

All we wanna do is,
All we wanna do is,
All we wanna do is SMASH!

Your road, our road,
Your shop, our shop,

Your car, our car,
And so what?

You shout, we shout,
You stare, we stare,
You start, we start,
Watch your back!

All we wanna do is... (*x3 repeated*)

SMASH!

*The sequence ends with the gang in a still image after having just thrown something through **Mr Jones'** window. They freeze as we hear the sound of breaking glass then they fall about laughing.*

Scar: 9 p.m., a Thursday night, we're on the estate . . .

Gang: Bored!

*They each step forward and introduce themselves as **Scar, Big Jay, Little Gee** and **Gaz**.*

Scar: Old man Jones at his window again.

Mr Jones: (*to audience*) Not that old. Sixty-two actually, could give them a run for their money.

*They all mimic **Mr Jones** as though peering through his window.*

Big Jay: He's doing that phone thing again, pretending to call the police . . . like we care anyway!

Gaz mimics a police officer.

Gaz: (*as police officer*) PC Riley, local community bobby.

Big Jay: Hello Dibble, long time, no see. Missed you like crazy.

Gaz: (*as police officer*) Name?

Big Jay: Tonight, Matthew, I'm going to be David Cameron.

Gaz: (*as police officer*) Right, you're coming with me son.

Big Jay: Phone my mam, tell her where I am, tell her to hurry up and bring me a butty – the food's crap at the station. About time you got that sorted, Dibble.

Gaz: (*as police officer*) Well excuse me, Gordon Ramsey! Don't get smart with me son.

Big Jay: I stopped being smart a long time ago officer. I ain't smart, nobody is round here.

Gang: And if you can't be smart, be bad!

You shout, we shout,
You stare, we stare,
You start, we start,
Watch your back!

Scene 2

Little Gee: On the estate, 9 p.m., Friday night. Old man Jones at his window again.

Scar: (*to* Mr Jones) What you looking at, then?

Gaz: Sad little man with nothing better to do.

Big Jay: Want a picture, do you?

Little Gee: (*to audience*) He's on our case every night.

Scar: Reckons we're harassing him.

Gaz: He reckons that we . . .

All: Disturb the peace!

Big Jay: What peace? You don't get any peace on an estate like this.

Gang: Halleluiah! Punch, kick, smash!

Mr Jones: (*to audience*) We've lived here all our married life, my wife and I. Used to be a lovely estate, quiet. Neighbours were decent people. We all knew each other, helped one another out when necessary, sometimes socialised but didn't make a habit of popping in and out of one another's houses. We liked it that way. Me and my wife are quite private people really, not keen on a lot of noise.

The gang are outside making as much noise as possible.

Mr Jones: (*to audience*) Things change, we accept that, but the way that this estate has changed, it's unbelievable. We're dictated to by yobs who think they own the place. My wall has become a central meeting point.

Scar: My wall that is, not yours, mine!

Gaz: (*mimicking* Mr Jones) You've got no right sitting there.

Big Jay: Move us then!

*We see **Mr Jones** coming out to move them and the gang take no notice, they refuse and become more intimidating.*

Scar:	Come on then, move us . . . Well come on, it is your wall after all.

Mr Jones *stops in his tracks.* **Gaz** *takes out a can of spray paint and begins to spray the words 'my wall' onto the wall.*

Gaz:	My wall, there we go, so there's no mistaking it now, is there?

Scene 3

Big Jay:	9 p.m., Saturday night. On the estate.
Gang:	Drinking.
Gaz:	'Cos that's what we like to do, and let's face it, what else is there to do round here to cheer you up?
Gang:	Way hey!
Gaz:	(*to imaginary passer-by*) Excuse me mate, will you go in there and get us some ale? Oh come on, you were underage once . . . yeah, well, cheers very much.

All give finger to passer-by as he walks away.

Little Gee:	What are we going to do now?
Big Jay:	We're out of cans.
Scar:	Well, they won't serve us in there, not after last time . . .
Gaz:	Yeah, when they asked Big Jay his age and he replied . . .
Gang:	Twenty-six!
Big Jay:	What's up with that?
Gaz:	(*mimicking the shopkeeper*) Does your mother know you're drinking?
Big Jay:	Does my mother care?
Gaz:	(*as shopkeeper*) What does she say when you get home drunk?
Big Jay:	(*mimicking his mum*) Don't be throwing up on me new IKEA rug. You bloody ruined my last one, carrots everywhere!
Gang:	Ew!
Gaz:	(*as shopkeeper*) Well, I think you'd better leave my shop young man and don't let me catch you asking for alcohol again. Is that clear?
Big Jay:	As mud.

Big Jay *mimes throwing something through the shop window.*

Big Jay:	(*shouting to shopkeeper*) Is that clear as well? Old cow!

Gaz: So no more corner shop purchases for us then. Where's Scar gone?

Scar: (*as though just running from his house*) I'm here. Got some booze from our house.

Gang: Smirnoff. Nice one. Down it, down it, down it!

They take long swigs and pass it down the line. When it gets to **Little Gee** *at the end he throws it into* **Mr Jones'** *garden.*

Mr Jones: (*to audience*) I watch them through a gap in the curtain, mucking around, wild like animals, and then to top it all the little vandals have the nerve to throw their litter into my garden.

Gaz: He appears, Mr Jones, face like thunder, and he starts . . .

Gang: Having a rant.

Mr Jones: (*to audience*) I'm shouting, ranting like a mad man and all they're doing is laughing in my face . . .

The lads are heckling him as he speaks.

Mr Jones: Pick that up, go on, pick it up, it's yours, you move it . . . I said move it – before I phone the police.

Gaz: Oh, not again, haven't you come up with something new yet? We're getting bored.

Mr Jones: (*to audience*) Truth is, I don't know what else to do, there are too many of them to confront. The police are sick to death of me moaning day after day. But what can I do, eh? It's my property, my garden, yet they use it as their dumping ground.

All: No respect for people or their property.

Mr Jones: (*to the lads*) I've got a sick wife in there.

Scar: There's a bit left in that vodka bottle, she's welcome to it, might cheer her up.

Gaz: Medicinal purposes!

Little Gee: Send her our best wishes, won't you?

Mr Jones: (*to audience*) I watch them walk away and I wonder how human beings can stoop so low. Dare I say it? 'What is the world coming to?'

Gang: Your night, our night
Your time, our time,
Your estate, our estate,
What you looking at?

Scene 4

Scar: 7 p.m., Sunday night, on his way out . . .

Gang: Gaz.

Scar: (*as mum's boyfriend*) 'Where are you going?' (*To audience, as Scar*), says mum's new fella.

Gaz: (*to audience*) Mum's big bastard bully of a boyfriend.

Scar: (*to audience*) Mum's on, off, never really been there, not a clue, doesn't give a damn, bully of a boyfriend. (*As boyfriend*) 'I'm talking to you, don't walk away from me when I'm talking to you! I said . . . (*Hits him*) . . . Where're you off?'

Gaz: (*timidly*) Out.

Scar: (*as boyfriend*) No you're not, you're stopping in with your brother.

Gaz: Where's me mam?

Scar: (*as boyfriend*) Like I should know, like I care.

Gaz: I'm not stopping in with him.

Scar: (*as boyfriend, he lunges towards him*) I ain't stopping in with him, I'm not your dad, you're not my problem.

Cut to other side of stage.

Little Gee: 7.30 p.m., Sunday night, on his way out . . .

Gang: Big Jay.

Little Gee: His mum says, as she necks the last dregs from the vodka bottle, (*As mum, drunk*) 'You going anywhere near the off-licence?'

Big Jay: No

Little Gee: (*as mum*) I need you to . . .

Big Jay: I said no, I'm not getting you any more booze – you're bladdered.

Little Gee: (*as mum*) I'm upset, you don't know what it's like for me. He's gone again, he's . . .

Big Jay: What? What what's like? Being bladdered day in and day out, and when you're not wasted, throwing up and then lying flat out on the couch . . . you're pathetic.

Little Gee: (*as mum*) Don't say that, I've given you everything . . .

Gang: You've given me nothing.

Big Jay: Sometimes I wonder why you even had me. Why did you bother?

Cut to **Gaz**.

Gaz: (*to audience*) Whose problem am I then?

Gang: I didn't ask to be born.

Cut back to **Big Jay**.

Little Gee: (*as mum*) I love you, I do my best . . .

Big Jay: This is your best?! This shit hole, this estate, this . . . (*Points to vodka bottle*) . . . I hate you!

Little Gee: (*as mum*) I love you . . . don't go, please just get me a drink . . .

Cut to **Gaz** *talking to imaginary brother.*

Gaz: I'm going out, you're staying here, don't touch anything, here's some crisps. When the video finishes it's bedtime . . . (*Turns back as if answering brother's question.*) well leave the light on then . . .

Cut back to **Big Jay**.

Big Jay: I hate you, I hate you!

Big Jay and Gaz: I hate you, I hate you!

Both run to front of stage as though running out of their houses onto the street.

Both: I hate you!

They slowly turn to face each other and then **Gaz** *turns towards* **Mr Jones'** *house.*

Gaz: I hate you, I hate him . . . what you looking at? (*He throws something at* Mr Jones' *house.*)

Gang: You shout, we shout,
You stare, we stare,
You start, we start,
Watch your back.

Scar: Bail!

Big Jay: (*to Gaz*) What happened to your face, Gaz?

Gang: (*slowly turn to face audience*) What happened?

Gaz: What happened to us?

Scene 5

Big Jay:	Scar's lived here all his life. He's out most nights. His mam says . . .
Gaz:	(*as mum*) Get out me face, go find something to do, get from under me feet.
Scar:	I'm not under your feet, wouldn't want to be, like pig's trotters, your feet.
Gaz:	(*as mum*) What was that? Wait till your dad gets home!
Scar:	I'll have a bloody long wait!
Little Gee:	But when he does go out there's nothing to do, so he looks for . . .
Scar:	Cars!

The lads mime stealing or vandalising a car.

Scar: (*sung to the tune of 'I like driving in my car'*)

I like wrecking people's cars,
It might not be a Jaguar.
A piece of scrap will do me fine,
Anything to pass the time.

And when I'm done with it, I trash it. Someone else's property? Nah, just a heap of metal really. They'll be insured, they'll get another one. A few dents and scratches, they'll soon get fixed. I guess that's why I hate cars. It's a love–hate relationship with them. I love the buzz, the feeling when I take them; I hate the fact they belong to someone else. Someone cares for that car and if they care enough they'll repair the dents and scratches. Not like human beings though, eh? No way you'll repair my dents and scratches. Scars that are the tell-tale signs of shitty lives. They call me Scar because of this (*He points to a scar on his head.*) They think I'm hard. I think I'm hard, except I know the truth. The scar won't heal, just like the memory. He hit me so hard they couldn't stop the bleeding. Can't forget . . . try to forget. 'Shhhh, it'll be OK, tell them you fell off your bike or I'll do it again.' Don't want to talk about it. Try to forget. Take it out on others, on the cars.

(Mr Jones *appears.*)

What do you want?

Mr Jones:	I saw you take that car.
Scar:	Well, can you see this? (*Holds a crowbar*) You'll be coming into very close contact with this soon if you keep on making accusations.

Mr Jones: That's no accusation, I saw you. You're a criminal.

Scar: What did you call me? I tell you what you are, you're a nosey old creep who's got nothing better to do with his time than stick his nose into everyone else's business. Watch your back old man, 'cos I'll be waiting for you. Keep an eye on that wife of yours as well, you never know what might happen when you're busy spying on others.

Mr Jones: (*to audience*) I open my mouth but the words don't come out. If only he knew. How could he bring her into it? You see she … Oh, what's the point?

Scene 6

Gaz: 9 p.m., Monday night …

Gang: Out on the estate.

All stare as if eyeballing an imaginary gang.

Gang: What you looking at? (*They look bored as the 'gang' walk away.*) Waiting.

Little Gee: For something to happen. Always waiting for something, never quite sure what. Waiting for me mam to get home and cook my tea, she doesn't. Waiting for my teachers to tell me that I did something good for once, but they don't. Waiting around the corner till the police have gone by, not wanting to be caught wagging school again.

Big Jay: No school anymore, didn't last long anywhere. Unruly, uncontrollable, and so what?

Gang: Watching.

Gaz: Watching other people trying to make the most of their tired, pathetic little lives when really they've got no hope, not on this estate.

Gang: Bored.

Scar: So we have to make our own entertainment.

Gang: Punch, kick, smash.

Scar: What are we going to do tonight?

Gaz: Never short of entertainment at the moment. Our eyes meet, we read each others' thoughts, our gaze turns to number thirty-six.

Gang:	Mr Jones.
Gaz:	At his window, spying on us, making sure we don't disturb his ordered little life. We're off, whatever we can do to taunt, goad, upset, provoke.
Big Jay:	Knock and run . . .
Little Gee:	Two fingers . . .
Scar:	Chucking stones . . .
Gaz:	Staring.
Big Jay:	Pointing.
Little Gee:	Shouting.
Scar:	Swearing.
Gaz:	On top of his wall . . .
Big Jay:	Over his wall . . .
Little Gee:	On his flower beds . . .
Mr Jones:	Not my flower beds, not my garden, please not the garden, she loves that garden, her only pleasure.
Scar:	Running up and down . . .
Gaz:	Laughing . . .
Big Jay:	Kicking soil everywhere . . .
Little Gee:	Flowers . . . (*To an imaginary passer-by*) for you, madam.
Scar:	Laughing harder now.
Gaz:	Chanting.
Gang:	Chanting, chanting, chanting, chanting.
Mr Jones:	Off my garden, get off!
Gang:	Off, off, off, off!
Mr Jones:	I said get off my garden, off, go on, move . . .
All:	Or I'll call the police.
Mr Jones:	This is my property, you've got no right.
Gaz:	Move us then . . . come on!
Gang:	Come on then, come on then, come on then, off, off, off . . .
Mr Jones:	(*to audience*) Head spinning, anger like I've never known before. I want to kill them, I just want to kill them, or me . . . no longer in control, being laughed at. This isn't me, I used to be so strong.

© 2014, *Learning about Social Issues through Scripts for Learners aged 11–16*, John Rainer and Kirsty Walters, Routledge

Gang: Off, off, off, off . . .

Gaz: Come on then, make us leave, old man, do something. (*To audience*) The feeling it gives you, the power, the control, we have it all . . . I have it all. No longer Gaz the lad who's so terrified of his mam's fella beating him into next week, no longer the little boy who cowers behind his bed, heart pounding, can't make a sound, can't let him find me. No longer the little lad who feels every punch and kick delivered. (*As if to mum's boyfriend*) 'Please, don't! I'm sorry'. No, none of that now, this is the real Gaz, he's hard, he's in control, he causes the suffering and it feels great.

Mr Jones: (*to audience*) They won't stop, it will never stop. Months of constant torture.

Gang: Chanting, chanting, chanting. Off, off, off.

Gaz: Don't want it to stop, won't let it stop . . . come on then!

Mr Jones goes back into the house and slams his front door behind him.

Gang: Slam, door shut. Way hey!

Scar: Come on lads, let's get out of here, we've won, got him that time. (*To* Gaz) Come on mate, let's go.

Gaz: (*staring at the door of number 36*) Behind that door . . .

Gaz and Mr Jones: . . . Is a broken man.

Mr Jones: (*to audience*) My heart won't stop racing, the anger is slowly disappearing and all I feel is pain, the pain of . . .

Mr Jones and Gaz: Humiliation.

Mr Jones: (*as if calling to his wife*) It's alright love, just some kids messing around, I sorted them out, got rid of them, gone now. I'm coming love.

Scene 7

Little Gee: 9pm, Tuesday night.

All: The night it happened.

Little Gee: Just another night of . . .

All: Taunting, shouting, goading, provoking.

Little Gee: I guess it's what we wanted, to push him as far as we could, to see how far he could be pushed.

Gang: You shout, we shout,
You stare, we stare,

> You start, we start,
> Watch your back!

Mr Jones: (*to audience*) It'd been quiet for a couple of nights. I really believed that this time they might have given up, how foolish can one be?

Big Jay: It was a laugh, just a laugh, we didn't mean any harm.

Gang: Yeah we did, course we did.

Big Jay: Well, maybe just a bit.

Mr Jones: (*to audience*) I'd settled down in front of the box, I'd made her comfortable, she'd just got off to sleep. Restful. Peaceful. Quiet. No stress.

Scar: Slowly we approach . . . Tonight we will see how far we can push him.

Gang: (*whisper*) You shout, we shout . . .

Mr Jones: (*to audience*) Quiet, rested, peaceful, a kind of calm . . .

Gang: (*shout*) Before the storm!

Gaz: Come on, it'll be a laugh.

Little Gee: I'm not sure.

Scar: Don't be soft, he deserves it, always on our backs.

Gaz: He won't even know it's us.

Big Jay: But he'll have a good idea. We'll make our mark, a trade mark, but he'll be able to prove nothing.

Scar: Moving slowly closer . . .

Little Gee: Preparing . . .

Gaz: Taking aim . . .

Big Jay: I hold up the brick, high up, taking aim.

Scar: Get ready to run.

Gang: (*A soundscape combining 'You shout, we shout', 'Monday night, Tuesday night . . .' and 'All we wanna do is . . .' It ends with all shouting, 'SMASH'*)

Mr Jones: (*to audience*) I jump up, glass everywhere, in front of the TV is a brick, and I know it's them. I'm outside and the cheek of them waiting to see my reaction. Glass shattered, my window. My wife cries out, what can I do? I have the brick in my hand, they turn to go, jeering. I hesitate for a second and then . . .

Gaz: He's chucking it.

Scar: Watch out!

They all watch and move in slow motion as it hits **Big Jay.** *He falls.*

Little Gee: You hit him! Jay, are you OK?

Gaz: You hit him, you bastard, you hit him.

Scar: You hit him!

Mr Jones: I hit him.

All stand as if in a court room. They place their right hands in front of them, as though swearing on the bible.

All: Guilty or not guilty? I swear to tell the truth, the whole truth and nothing but the truth . . .

Big Jay: Nothing but the truth.

Scene 8

Mr Jones: (*to audience*) In the witness stand after months and months of more torture. A man on trial, in the stand. I try to explain, but I'm the criminal now, aren't I? I assaulted a young lad, I knocked him out cold, thought he was dead.

Gaz: He wasn't moving, just lying there.

Little Gee: There was blood, loads of it.

Gang: It wasn't even us that threw the brick, we were just there.

Scar: He blamed us for everything, he saw us there and . . .

Gang: Presumed it was us.

Scar: But it wasn't, we didn't chuck any brick.

Gang: No not us, it wasn't us. Halleluiah!

Mr Jones: You have no idea what it was like, day in and day out, it went on for months. I just wanted it to stop.

Gaz: (*as prosecution*) So you took the law into your own hands.

Mr Jones: I was pushed. I just wanted it to stop. It's my wife, you see . . .

Gaz: (*as prosecution*) And so, Mr Jones, you decided to take action, to do something quick, to put an end to it?

Mr Jones: Yes, that's it, that's right.

Gaz: (*as prosecution*) So you violently assaulted a 15-year-old boy, not even certain that he was in fact the perpetrator of the crime committed against your window. You were not thinking straight, were you, Mr Jones? You were intent upon revenge . . .

Mr Jones: No . . . I mean, yes . . . I mean . . . You're not listening to me . . . my life was being destroyed!

Gang: And so you took the law into your own hands.

Mr Jones: No, I just wanted it to stop.

Gang: You just wanted it to stop

Mr Jones: That's right.

Gang: You assaulted a 15-year-old child.

Mr Jones: Yes . . . I mean, no . . . I mean . . .

The lads become the voices of the public or press.

A: That man was pushed to the limit.

B: He should never have taken the law into his own hands.

C: Taunted and tortured.

D: But he assaulted an innocent child.

Gang: (*to audience, with confused facial expressions*) Innocent!

Mr Jones: Those kids were far from innocent. They were intent upon destroying my life. They intimidated.

Gaz: Goaded.

Scar: Taunted.

Little Gee: Tormented.

Big Jay: Destroyed. I watched him there in the stand. We sat in the gallery above. The others jeered at times, but not me, I'd done enough. There in the stand he looked like an old man, he looked . . .

Mr Jones: Tired, shattered . . . Guilty. Yes, guilty. I threw the brick at him, I did that, but you must understand . . .

Gang: Justice.

Mr Jones: I just wanted it to stop, my property, my garden, my window smashed . . .

Gang: Justice.

Mr Jones: My wife, you see . . . I had to protect her . . .

All: Justice.

Mr Jones: She has cancer.

(*Pause*)

She can't fight it anymore. They say there's nothing they can do. I had to protect her, it was the least I could do. She couldn't fight anymore.

We go to a flashback of the vodka bottle scene.

Mr Jones: I've got a sick wife in there.

Scar: There's a bit left in this bottle, she's welcome to it, might cheer her up.

Gaz: Medicinal purposes!

Little Gee: Send her our best wishes, won't you?

Mr Jones: She just couldn't fight anymore, I couldn't fight anymore . . . I shouldn't have done it I know that, but . . .

Gang: Guilty or not guilty?

A soundscape of chants from the play is built up as we see **Mr Jones** *slowly collapse to the floor.*

Big Jay: Guilty. I had never felt such guilt in my life before. We watched him fall to the ground, his face contorted with pain, clutching his heart, slowly life was draining away. We had done that.

Other lads: He got what he deserved . . . (*They stare at the audience to suggest doubt.*)

Big Jay: They said it was a heart attack.

Gaz: Couldn't take the strain.

Little Gee: The stress of it all.

They slowly walk forward whispering 'Your life, our life'. They stop suddenly when Big Jay says his next line.

Big Jay: Who'll look after her now? His wife, I mean . . .

Music is played throughout the final sequence. **Big Jay** *slowly walks towards an imaginary front door at the front of the stage, he is holding some flowers. He mimes knocking on the door and then speaks to an imaginary person who has opened the door.*

Big Jay: I brought these for Mrs Jones, could you give them to her please? Please take them, please . . .

The other lads quietly whisper 'please' as the lights fade to a spotlight where the flowers are placed.

PATHWAY 1: KS3 – AN EXPLORATORY APPROACH FOR YOUNGER LEARNERS

Pathway 1 workshops provide an opportunity for learners to explore the issues raised by the play, clarify their values and express their responses in dramatic form – relating to their own experiences. There are also opportunities for 'thinking skills' to be developed; for instance, through the use of Edward De Bono's six *thinking hats,* whereby the colours of each hat represent a particular perspective on a problem or issue, or a specific type of thinking.

The workshops also provide the opportunity to develop literacy skills, as learners are encouraged to work with the script and produce some of their own writing. The main aim of the Pathway 1 units is to provide learners with a greater awareness of the issues surrounding the play: the unit and play can therefore be used as a basis for cross-curricular work addressing aspects of citizenship, literacy and PSHE.

Workshop 1: What is meant by antisocial behaviour, and what are its causes and consequences?

Resources needed for this workshop

Copies of the letter written by Amy Newlove to her father Garry, or a projection of the letter: http://image.guardian.co.uk/sys-images/Guardian/Pix/pictures/2007/08/14/newloveletter.jpg

Large sheets of paper and pens for the 'thinking hats' task.

Resource sheet of facts surrounding the Newlove case.

ASB factsheet.

'True', 'False' and 'Unsure' captions.

Learners enter the space and are presented with a projection or caption of the phrase 'Antisocial behaviour', and the question, 'what is antisocial behaviour?'

After one minute of thinking time, ask group members to turn to the person next to them and share their ideas for a further minute.

From this, bring the group together and discuss their ideas on the definition of antisocial behaviour and the types of behaviour that might be regarded as antisocial.

The captions 'True', 'False' and 'Unsure' are then positioned around the space and students are asked to move to the appropriate caption in response to a series of facts, read by the group leader (Resource sheet 1).

The group is brought back together and asked to reflect on the 'facts' presented. Have they learnt anything new, or have their opinions been challenged in any way?

Summarise for the group the range of activities that are regarded in law as antisocial – from dropping litter or writing graffiti, to serious acts of violence. It is also important to highlight the kinds of sanctions that the law uses against those prosecuted for ASB. In order to illustrate an extreme example of the consequences of antisocial behaviour, read to the group the letter written by the then 12-year-old Amy Newlove to her father Garry, who was in a coma after having been attacked outside his house by a group of teenage boys. For greater impact, project the actual letter for learners to study. Do not, at this point, reveal the fact that Garry Newlove died as a result of the attack.

Ask the group to consider:

- What might have happened?
- What might have led up to this series of events?

After a short discussion, reveal the 'facts' of the case and allow learners time to reflect on the new information (Resource sheet 2).

Learners are now placed in groups of four or five and are allocated a large sheet of paper, a pen and particular 'colour' – white, black, yellow, red or green. De Bono's *thinking hats* are now used to explore different perspectives on antisocial behaviour. Each group is asked to consider the general issue of antisocial behaviour from the perspective of their given 'colour'. For example, the 'red team' will consider the kinds of feelings generated by antisocial behaviour, whereas the 'yellow team' will consider if there are any 'positives' that may emerge. (See above for further explanation of *thinking hats*.) Ask each group to share two or three points raised in their discussion so that all learners are able to consider each perspective on the issue.

Using the ideas accumulated from the previous task, each group now adopts the role of a specialist team brought together to find a solution to the problem of antisocial behaviour affecting their community.

Their task is to present their 'action plan' to the local council. The action plan should illustrate the types of problem behaviour prevalent in the community and its consequences, as well as their suggested solution. Groups will need consider how they might choose to present their work 'to the council'. For example, some may enact examples of ASB, and the consequences, together with their favoured solution, others may simply 'pitch' their ideas, ensuring that each team member has a role in the presentation.

Each group is given the opportunity to present their work to the rest of the class ('the council'), who are able to decide on the most realistic solutions offered. What issues are raised by the presentations in relation to crime, punishment and community? These ideas and questions will be revisited throughout the following unit of work.

We acknowledge that this workshop is quite discursive, but our experience is that students are very keen to discuss their own experiences and voice their own opinions on the issues surrounding antisocial behaviour. It is vital for what follows that learners gain an understanding of the broad issues surrounding antisocial behaviour; we recommend that the introductory activities are kept brisk, with a lively pace maintained, so as to ensure sufficient time is allocated to the final two activities.

Extended learning

What kinds of activities might fall into the category of *antisocial behaviour*? Research any recent cases in the local area that may have been in the media.

Ensure that learners complete this task in preparation for the following workshop.

Resource sheet 1: Antisocial behaviour quiz

1. Antisocial behaviour is only carried out by young people. (True/False)

2. The issue of antisocial behaviour does not affect everyone in the community. (True/False)

3. The following types of behaviour are regarded as antisocial:

   a) Graffiti (True/False)

   b) Abusive and intimidating language (True/False)

   c) Excessive noise (True/False)

   d) Anything that annoys me (True/False)

   e) Dropping litter (True/False)

   f) Drunken behaviour (True/False)

   g) Dealing drugs (True/False)

   h) Making nuisance phone calls (True/False)

   i) Cycling on the footpath (True/False)

   j) Children playing in the street or communal areas or socially gathering. (True/False)

4. Antisocial behaviour is defined in law as 'behaviour which causes, or is likely to cause, harassment, alarm or distress to one or more people who are not in the same household as the perpetrator'. (True/False)

5. It is estimated that antisocial behaviour costs the British taxpayer £3.4bn a year. (True/False)

Answers to antisocial behaviour quiz

1. False.
2. False.
3. a) True , b) True, c) True, d) False, e) True, f) True, g) True, h) True, i) True, j) False.
4. True.
5. True.

Resource sheet 2: The murder of Garry Newlove

The attack took place on 10 August 2007, a Friday evening.

There was a history of trouble on the housing estate; the Newlove's next-door neighbour had recently installed CCTV in an attempt to discourage local youths. This camera later captured Garry Newlove going out of his house to speak to a group of teenagers.

The attack took place shortly after the gang had kicked his wife's car, parked outside their home.

Garry Newlove died two days later from serious head injuries.

Three teenagers, aged between 16 and 19, were convicted and jailed for the attack.

They received life sentences, and the judge recommended minimum prison sentences of between 12 and 17 years.

It emerged, after the three were found guilty, that the ringleader of the group had been released from custody for an assault just hours before the attack on 10 August. He had been freed on bail on condition he stayed away from Warrington, but he remained in the town despite the court order.

© 2014, *Learning about Social Issues through Scripts for Learners aged 11–16*,
John Rainer and Kirsty Walters, Routledge

Workshop 2: Exploring the opening of the play using a range of drama strategies

> **Resources needed for this workshop**
>
> Scenes 1, 2 and 3 of the play *ASBO.*
>
> Key **drama strategies** prompt sheets placed around the room.
>
> Checklist of strategies to give to each group.

'My fact is...'

Learners stand in the circle and share the information they found about antisocial behaviour for homework. They then point to another student in the circle who must also now share their facts.

After recapping on what was learnt in the previous workshop, read the opening scenes of the play (Scenes 1, 2 and 3).

Key questions are:

- What exactly is happening on the estate?
- What do you think about the way Mr Jones is dealing with this behaviour?
- Why do you think the boys choose to behave the way they do?

Learners are now asked to consider ways of setting the scene. Reference could be made here to *drama strategies prompt sheets*, which are placed around the room.

- Where is this scene set?
- How could the scene be established in a way that will create atmosphere, mood or tension?
- What information is important to communicate to the audience in the opening scene?
- Which characters need to be in the opening scene?

The class is now split into small groups and each is allocated one verse from the opening chant in the play (see p. 7). Their task is to find an interesting way of presenting their verse, which is then performed by the whole class by presenting each verse in turn.

Groups are now asked to develop their pieces by folding in the opening dialogue, which captures the essence of what is happening on the estate. A checklist of strategies could again be highlighted to prompt ideas.

Learners share and evaluate the work, using the checklist as prompts for evaluative comment. As a technique to encourage self-assessment they then move to an area of the room marked with a label – a drama skill or strategy that they think they have used well in the workshop. Once choices have been made, encourage learners to justify how and why they have used that particular strategy or skill in their drama.

Extended learning

Complete *learner's logs* (see Box 1.1).

Workshop 3: The characters' lives and their motivation and function in the play

---

Resources needed for this workshop

School bag, mobile phone, exercise book (and any other props that might be found in the bag of one of the gang).

Paper and pens.

Scenes 4 and 5 of the play *ASBO*.

A school bag is placed centre stage and the class are informed that it belongs to one of the characters in the play. The contents of the bag are slowly revealed: a mobile phone, a can of coke, a pair of trainers, a scruffy exercise book, etc.

Learners are asked to consider what the 'clues' in the bag tell us about the character that owns it. Ask them to think particularly about the phone, and what information it could give us.

Think time

What *text message* could be on the phone to provide information or insight about this character?

The class is now told that the exercise book found in the bag contains further information that reveals more about the character. Learners are asked to work alone and, on paper provided, write down what they imagine to be in the back of the exercise book.

Some learners then share their work whilst others consider what the writing might convey or reveal about the character.

The class now read Scenes 4 and 5 of the play.

In pairs, learners are asked to choose one character from the play. Once they have made their choice, identify other characters who do not appear in the script but could possibly have interacted with their first character.

Anti-social behaviour

Each pair is now asked to choose the 'unseen' character with most dramatic potential, and improvise a situation where the two meet and interact.

Key questions to consider are:

- Where and when is the scene set?
- What is the action of the scene, and what might the characters talk about?
- What might be said that reveals the character's motivation or reveals insight into their state of mind?

Whilst pairs are rehearsing, the teacher chooses a group of 'mentors' who go from group to group listening and advising other groups on how they might improve their work.

Learners share and discuss the scenes. Mentors evaluate using *what went well?/Even better if . . .*, and then feed back their thoughts.

Extended learning

Complete *learner's logs* or create a *diary entry* as a character explored in today's workshop.

Workshop 4: From 'page to stage'

Resources needed for this workshop

Scenes 5 and 6 of the play *ASBO*.

Paper and pens.

Read Scenes 5 and 6, stopping to discuss any issues raised.

Having read the two scenes, focus the group's attention on Scene 6 and ask them to consider any problems that may arise in staging it.

Ask them to consider:

- What is the main *action* of the scene?
- The *pace* of the scene; are there variations in pace and tempo?
- Where is the *climax* of the scene? How might this be emphasised?
- How might space be used best to make the scene effective?

Learners are placed into groups of five or six and are asked to experiment with ways of presenting the scene. One group member may wish to take on the role of the director during this task.

Share and evaluate the different versions performed.

Each group is now asked to write their own script which shows what happened on another night not mentioned in the play. It may be helpful to split each group so that they work in twos or threes on this task.

Once learners have completed their own scene they are asked to swap with another group and work on interpreting and presenting this new script.

Learners will then perform their scene and the writers of that particular script will be given an opportunity to discuss whether or not the scene was interpreted in the way that they had intended.

Extended learning

Complete *learner's logs* or script their own enhanced scene.

Workshop 5: Exploring characters' emotions on the night of the attack

Resources needed for this workshop

Copies of Scene 7 of the play *ASBO*.

Read Scene 7 of the play, which describes events on the night of the attack.

The class take part in a *relay hot-seat* to further explore the events of that night. Key questions are:

- What emotions might each character experience immediately after the attack?
- How might an actor convey such emotion?
- Can the group suggest a drama strategy or technique that a director could employ to further communicate the emotion of that night?

Ask groups to prepare a scene that depicts the 30 seconds of action after the brick is thrown (after the line 'You hit him!'). Explain that the strategy of *cross-cutting* could be used here to explore two different/contrasting viewpoints.

Watch some of the pieces and discuss how *emotion* and *tension* were created in the scenes.

Now ask learners to develop another piece which shows what could have happened two hours later. How do emotions change? Does the pace differ? How does this scene contrast with the first?

Share and evaluate the work.

Extended learning

Complete *learner's logs.*

Workshop 6: Exploring different 'sides' and perspectives to the story

> **Resources needed for this workshop**
>
> Copies of Scene 8 of the play *ASBO*.

Read the final scene of the play, the *courtroom scene.*

Think time

Learners are asked to use *'green hat' thinking*: were there any alternatives to what happened? What 'solutions' were there to this situation?

Place a chair in the centre of the space to represent Big Jay and ask volunteers to take up a position somewhere around it. Where and how they stand in the room should reflect how they might feel about Big Jay.

Ask learners to consider who the volunteers in the space might represent.

Thought-track the volunteers to gain further insight.

Ask the rest of the class to join the 'picture' and take up a position around the chair. They must also portray a character that has an opinion about Big Jay.

Index cards are placed on the floor nearby each student, and they are asked to write a *mini-monologue* in role as that character. The teacher might like to model this first.

Learners are now put into smaller groups and some are asked to read their monologues to the rest of the class or to the person next to them (their *learning buddy*).

They are now asked to create a piece of drama in which the monologues could be linked and turned into a performance. The piece must contain each person's point of view, a link between each monologue and a variety of other strategies that could enhance the piece.

Extended learning

Learner's log entry.

Workshop 7: Presenting non-naturalistic drama based on Big Jay's thoughts and feelings

> **Resources needed for this workshop**
>
> Music.
>
> Lighting.
>
> Copy of the 'doctor's report'.

Learners are asked to consider why Big Jay takes the flowers to Mr Jones' wife at the end of the play. What is his motivation? What might be his nightmare – the thing he fears most?

The whole class creates a *conscience alley* to explore the thoughts and feelings in Big Jay's head as he walks to Mr Jones' house with the flowers for his wife.

In small groups, learners are asked to devise a *non-naturalistic* scene which shows Big Jay's nightmare or the thoughts in his head. Learners may be given strategies to use; for example, a series of *still images* and a *soundscape,* or they could be given the opportunity to experiment with a variety of strategies of their own choice.

Share and evaluate the work.

Extended learning

A *learner's log* entry, or written account of how learners presented the thoughts in Big Jay's head, or group members photograph their own work which can be mounted with a *thought bubble* containing their own 'spoken thoughts'.

Learner's log

It is up to the teacher how often learners are asked to complete learner's logs. It may be appropriate to complete an entry every lesson, or when the teacher sees that it may help extend and consolidate learning.

PATHWAY 2: KS4 – A PERFORMANCE-SKILLS APPROACH FOR OLDER LEARNERS

Each Pathway 2 workshop is structured in such a way that it encourages all learners to take responsibility for their own learning through independent enquiry, problem solving, assessment for learning and thinking skills approaches. Workshops are much less teacher-led than in KS3; however, they do require teacher intervention at various stages (particularly at the start of each workshop).

The structure of each workshop is as follows:

- *Building blocks*: starters that are mostly teacher-led tasks which equip learners with the skills or information required for the challenge.
- *The challenge*: the main focus/task in the workshop.
- *Top tips/Ask the expert*: During this phase learners are required to 'buddy up' and peer-assess one another's work.
- *Re-focus and refine*: During this phase learners are required to alter their thinking process and consider their work from one or more new perspectives. They are then given the opportunity to adapt or develop their work.

Workshop 1: Monologues

> **Resources needed for this workshop**
>
> Paper and coloured pens.
>
> Copies of Scene 5 of the play *ASBO*.

Building blocks

Read Scar's monologue (Scene 5).

- Discuss the purpose of monologue as a performance and as a play-building strategy.
- Ask learners to take up a position in the space and think of a character (who may or may not be in the play) who could in some way be linked to Scar. For example, his mum, dad, social worker, friend, a neighbour, Mrs Jones . . .). Learners are then thought-tracked in role as that character.
- To expand upon this, learners now take part in *mix, pair, share*. When the teacher shouts *mix* they must move through the space in role as their chosen

character. When the teacher shouts *pair* learners stop opposite someone closest to them and make eye contact. When the teacher shouts *share* learners share an exchange in role as their character. This could be a brief conversation role played between the two.

- Learners are now asked to consider how spoken thoughts could be expanded into monologues and what their purpose might be.

The challenge

Learners must create a monologue in role as their chosen character. It must give insight into the character's emotional state and include a revelation of some kind. This then needs to be recorded in written form.

Top tips/Ask the expert

Learners now share their monologue with a partner who must provide feedback and constructive criticism. Partners then suggest stage directions to enhance their partner's monologue; these can be highlighted on the 'script'.

Re-focus and refine

Learners now practise performing their monologues in different ways in order to explore different avenues of performance:

- Perform without speech
- Static with no movement or gesture
- Sitting down
- 'Over the top' gesture for every line
- Repeat the same line over and over in a different way
- Speak it very quickly or very slowly.

After this exercise learners are given the opportunity to develop or adapt their monologues and add in new stage directions.

Learners may wish to perform their work to their peers.

Workshop 2: Devising

> **Resources needed for this workshop**
>
> Paper and pens.
>
> Drama strategy cards.

Building blocks: Life beyond the play

Learners are asked to consider the 'unwritten' scenes in the play and in small groups jot down as many ideas as they can think of. In these groups learners are asked to choose one of these moments and improvise a short scene based on it. Groups may like to share their work with another group.

Key strategies are placed around the room on large pieces of card, for example *role play, spoken thought, narration, still image, cross-cutting.* The teacher reads out a series of definitions and learners move to the strategy that they think is being described. This is a good way of revising and checking student knowledge and understanding. Learners are asked to consider how they could use any of these strategies as stepping stones to building their unseen scene.

The challenge

The next task is to devise an unseen scene from the play, incorporating two or more of the strategies explored during the previous task.

Top tips/Ask the expert

Each group combines with another group and shows their piece. The group who observes must evaluate and offer suggestions for improvement.

Re-focus and refine

Groups are asked to show an excerpt from their piece to the whole class and answer one of the following questions (which are placed in a bag and picked out one per group):

- Why did you choose this moment?
- What strategies have you incorporated and why?
- What is the most entertaining/dramatic moment in your piece and why?
- What would you improve if given more time?

Each group is then given the opportunity to alter/develop their scene and share it with the rest of the group.

Workshop 3: Approaches to characterisation

Resources needed for this workshop

Character, purpose, motivation chart.

Pens and paper.

Key words cards.

Tick list of characterisation techniques and skills.

Slips of paper with characters' names.

Building blocks

The class read Scene 3 together, using volunteers to read certain roles.

- In groups of five, learners are asked to experiment with presenting a section of the scenes. They must each take on one key role.
- Some groups may wish to perform their short scene.
- The group are now asked to discuss what is meant by *purpose, motivation* and *character*. They are each given a chart with the above words as headings for each column. Each student is asked to complete the chart based on the character they have just played (Table 1.1).

Table 1.1

Character	Purpose	Motivation

The group now reconvene and take part in a game of *My Character Is ...*

Learners stand in a circle. One student begins by saying 'My character is ...' and then they complete the sentence by giving some background information based on that character. Once they have done this, they point to someone else in the circle who must repeat the exercise. This provides learners with an opportunity to vocalise what they know or interpret about their character.

Learners are now encouraged to explore their characters further by taking part in a *relay hot-seating* task. One by one, learners sit in the hot seat and must answer some quick-fire questions in role as their character.

The group are now asked to consider the actor's skills needed when portraying a role. Key words placed down in the centre of the circle as prompt cards may be helpful; for example, *voice, movement, gesture, body language, facial expression, spoken language.*

Learners are now asked to complete a *character map*, where they record their response to each of the key words.

The challenge

In pairs, learners must adopt the role of one key character from the play and create a scene in which these two characters could meet. The main focus of this task is to create a thoroughly convincing portrayal of the chosen (or given) character. The teacher may also like to suggest possible scenarios in which these characters could meet – for example, in hospital, at the school gates or in twenty years' time.

Top tips/Ask the expert

Each pair combines with another in order to present their work. The observers are asked to complete a tick list of characterisation techniques as they see them occur, and comment on their effectiveness (Table 1.2).

Table 1.2

Skill	Comment
Voice	
Body language	
Gesture	
Facial expression	
Spoken language	
Movement	

Re-focus and refine

Learners are now asked to experiment with various ways of playing their characters. The teacher leads this exercise and gives the following instructions:

- Play the scene without dialogue
- 'Over the top'
- Fast-paced
- As though in a confined space
- As though across a busy street
- As though in secret
- In an agitated manner
- Aggressively
- As though numb – with no emotion.

Once learners have completed this exercise they should be asked to consider the effect of the various approaches. Did any of them suggest a way forward in playing the scene? Which challenged them the most?

Learners are now given the opportunity to adapt or develop their pieces and the way in which they portray their characters.

They may wish to share and evaluate their work at the end of the session.

Workshop 4: Script writing

> **Resources needed for this workshop**
>
> Character table.
>
> Paper and pens.

Building blocks

Ask each group to choose one of the main characters in the play.

Get them to think of possible 'scenes' which might have taken place between this character and one or two other people who are not characters in the play but might be referred to (examples might be Scar's father, or Gaz's brother).

From their initial ideas, ask each group to fill in a table (Table 1.3).

Table 1.3

Who? (main character)	
Who with? (other characters)	
When? (in relation to the action of the play: past, present or future?)	
Where? (location of the scene)	
Doing what? (why are the characters there?)	

Once they have completed the tables, give the learners time to improvise what might have happened in the encounter between the characters. Encourage them to stop, and re-work the scene if things go wrong, and to record parts of their improvisation that they are pleased with. If the groups struggle to improvise the scene without support, give them time to *hot seat* each other in character.

The challenge

Learners must create a short script based upon their improvisations. It must develop our understanding of the main character in some way, and must end with a *freeze* at a moment of high dramatic tension.

Top tips/Ask the expert

Learners now swap their scripts with another group, who attempt to stage it for performance. After working time, groups perform the script extracts to each other, feed back to each other on the problems they encountered and give suggestions for how the scripts might be improved.

Re-focus and refine

Groups receive their original scripts back and refine them.

If time allows, the scripts can be performed to the whole group. The key evaluative question is, 'how did the additional scene help us to understand the character better?'

Workshop 5: Staging the play for performance

> **Resources needed for this workshop**
>
> Scene 4 of the play *ASBO*.

Building blocks

Read Scene 4, which uses some interesting staging techniques and presents particular 'multi-rolling' challenges to actors. Ask the group what problems they would need to solve in order to stage the scene successfully. Suggestions might include:

- *Stepping in and out of character* – for instance, as Scar at the beginning of the scene when he 'becomes' Mum's boyfriend, and then the line after when he addresses the audience as himself again.
- *Cross-cutting* from parallel scenes in separate stage locations
- 'Choreographing' the lines when all characters speak in unison.

Ask for suggestions as to how the staging problems they identify might be resolved.

The challenge

Working in groups of four, the task is to stage the scene so that it can be performed to the rest of the group, with scripts, but fluently so that:

- All cast members can be seen at all times (no 'blocking')
- Actors switch clearly from one character to another
- The audience's attention is focused on 'where the action is' during the cross-cutting sections
- The actors are able to realise the dramatic effect of the parts delivered in unison.

Top tips/Ask the expert

Ask each group to 'pair up' with another and perform their (work-in-progress) scenes to each other; each group should give detailed feedback on how far they have succeeded in the four elements of the challenge, and how they might improve their work.

Re-focus and refine

Groups then work to create a more polished version of the scene based on the feedback they have received before final performances are shared with the whole group.

Workshop 6: Enhancing the work with technology

Resources needed for this workshop

Slideshow of images relating to the play's themes.

Digital cameras and computers with presentation software.

Eight-frame story boards.

Building blocks

Present the group with a slideshow of images that relate in some way to the play's theme. Examples might be newspaper headlines, images of young people – but take care not to stereotype too much, and to select positive as well as negative images of young people and events.

Ask the group to study the slideshow and to note down any images which, when projected onto a screen as a backdrop, they think might add something to the play. They might relate directly to the themes or characters of the play, or resonate with a particular moment or emotion generated within a scene.

Run the slideshow again and ask each student to indicate which images they selected, and discuss why they selected them.

- Which images were 'most popular'?
- Why did people choose those particular images?
- Would they work best at particular moments in the play, or a *prologue* or *epilogue*?
- What effect might they have on the play's audience – how would the play be enhanced?
- How far do the images they have chosen reinforce, or subvert, the stereotypical image of 'feral' youth?

The challenge

Working in pairs and using digital cameras, the challenge is to create a slideshow of eight images which might serve as an introduction to the play in performance.

Provide the class with an eight-frame storyboard which they can use to plan their picture sequence. Tell them that they can research images from the media in order to stimulate ideas, but that the actual images used must be created by the learners themselves.

Ask them to consider the following:

- Are the images going to depict actual characters or events from the play?
- Are the images intended to provide context – or setting – for the action of the play?
- Are they going to use abstract or literal images, or a mixture?
- Are the images going to try to 'comment' in some way on the play?
- Does altering the order – chronology – of the images, once selected, alter the 'meaning' of the sequence?

Top tips/Ask the expert

Once they have completed the storyboard exercise, ask each pair to join with another and take turns in presenting their ideas. Encourage the groups to justify the choices they have made.

Re-focus and refine

Groups now work with digital cameras to create their eight images, and then upload them into presentation software.

Once the work is complete, share and evaluate. Ask each pair to identify the most effective sequences and individual images. Can they say why they worked best? How might they affect the audience's understanding of the play?

Eating disorders

Introduction and context

It is estimated that 1.6 million people in the UK have an eating disorder, and that 1 in 5 sufferers is male. Information from The National Health Service suggests that there has been a 66 per cent increase in hospital admissions in England for male eating disorders over the last ten years. Statistics reveal that males may account for 1–5 per cent of patients with anorexia nervosa, although prior to puberty the risk increases and approximately 50 per cent of sufferers in children are boys.

This play, and the work based around it, was a response to a whole-school healthy eating initiative, and evolved into a GCSE devising project, taking as its focus the issue of eating disorders and body image but from a male perspective. This gave opportunities to get into something of a taboo area – the more we researched, the more we found a gap in information on young males with eating disorders. This play explores the pressures on young men to look right and 'fit in'. Darren's story highlights how quickly an eating disorder can spiral out of control and the impact that it can have on those around the 'victim'. In doing so, working on the play opened up an important discussion – amongst both boys and girls – about their self-image and the pressures placed on teenagers to look a certain way. It deserves to be taken beyond the drama classroom, and clear links are made with PSHE and other curriculum areas.

Waisted – The play

A note from the playwright

The play was written to complement the 'Healthy Schools' initiative currently in secondary schools in the UK at the time of writing. The issues explored regarding body image and eating disorders could also be used alongside PSHE lessons.

The play tells the story of 15-year-old Darren Thomas who dreams of becoming a top footballer. However, his obsession with getting 'into shape' gets dangerously out of hand . . .

KW

Waisted

Kirsty Walters

Cast

Darren Thomas
   (otherwise known as 'Daz'):   A 16-year-old footballer
Sue Thomas: Darren's mum, 36 yrs
Mac: Darren's dad and the coach of a local football team, 39 yrs
Callum: Darren's younger brother, 12 yrs
Jenny
   (otherwise known as 'Jen'):   Darren's girlfriend, 15 yrs
Helen: Jenny's mum, 41 yrs
Kate: Jenny's best friend, 15 yrs
Wayne: Darren's best friend and Jenny's brother, 16 yrs
Doctor Barker: The family GP

Scene 1

Lights come up on the cast, who are positioned centre stage. In slow motion they raise their heads and perform various movements to represent actions at a football match. A soundtrack of football crowds and a commentary can be heard in the background. Eventually the cast move into a 'V' shape and simultaneously move their heads from right to left and then central. All lean forward as if staring into a mirror, they touch their faces and then lower their hands to their stomachs. The music cuts and the cast disperse. The pace automatically quickens as we move to **Jenny's** *house. The cast become the voices of the family and create the chaos in the household saying lines such as* '**Wayne**, *have you moved my straighteners?',* '**Daz** *is here,* **Jen**', *'Won't be a minute . . .'*

Daz: (*to audience*) Daz, 16, Jen's boyfriend.

Daz and Jen: Captain of the school football team.

Jen: (*to audience*) Well fit, all my mates are dead jealous.

Girls: Yeah right!

Jen: (*to audience*) He asked me out in the most romantic of ways.

Daz: Do you want to then?

Jen: Yeah ok.

Helen:	(*to audience*) And that was that, who said romance was dead? Nice lad though.
Jen:	(*to audience*) Me and my mum talk about everything, she knew how much I fancied him.
Helen:	If it's meant to be … how much make-up have you got on lady?
Daz:	(*to* Helen) Alright, Mrs M?
Helen:	Hiya love … don't be bringing any mud into this house, I've got enough bloody mess on this carpet, don't know why I bother putting a rug down, nobody uses it …
Jen:	Mother!
Helen:	Never mind 'Mother'!
Daz:	It's fine, I'll take them off.
Jen:	Don't bother, we're going now.
Wayne:	(*to audience*) Cue Jen's older brother, Wayne, aged 16. (*To* Daz) Hiya Daz, you been playing footie?
Daz:	Yeah, just been training, got a match tomorrow.
Wayne:	Fancy a kick about?
Jen:	No he doesn't, we're off out.
Helen:	And you've got homework to finish and a shower to have. He doesn't come here to entertain you.
Jen:	He's taking me out.
Daz:	Sorry mate, that'll be a 'no' then!
Helen:	Will you both be wanting tea?
Jen:	Nah, we'll grab a burger while we're out.
Helen:	(*to audience*) Bloody burger mad!

Scene 2

All:	A scene change. Jen's favourite hobby, shopping.
	The cast use body as props to become the clothes rails.
Jen:	(*as though holding up a top*) Now that is gorgeous. What do you think? I could wear this on Friday.
Daz:	I thought you'd already got your outfit planned.
Jen and Rail:	Well, a girl can change her mind you know.
Rail:	£23.99, go great with a pair of skinny jeans, very this season … no pressure.

Jen:	Should I try it on?
Daz:	Whatever.
Jen:	Are you trying anything else on?
Daz:	Nah.
Jen:	What about those jeans, are you getting them?
Daz:	They didn't look right.

The rails become the changing cubicles.

Shop assistant (played by Helen): (*as if talking to lots of different customers*) One free just at the end, sorry about the wait, got a girl who's been in there forty minutes, can't find the right thing for a wedding.

All: Now't to fit her.

Girl (played by Kate): I didn't say that. I'm just big boned.

Shop assistant: A minute on the lips, a lifetime on the hips. Last Saturday we had a woman in there two hours.

Jen: Trying stuff on?

Shop assistant: No, she'd passed out in the heat – but when you're busy you just don't realise. One free for you at the end, on the right.

A few seconds later **Jen** *appears as if wearing the top.*

Jen: What do you think?

Daz and shop assistant: Nice.

Jen: I look well fat, don't I? Does it pull?

Daz: It's fine, you're not fat.

Shop assistant: If you think you're fat I've got no chance.

We hear a soundscape of the other girls in the changing room commenting, 'There's nothing on her', 'Well skinny. . .'

Jen: (*as if coming out of the changing room*) That is so not a size 8!

All girls: The lighting is terrible in there.

Daz: Are you getting it then?

Jen: I looked well fat in it.

Daz: Did you?

Jen: (*to the clothes rail*) Here, you can have it back.

Rail: A wise decision, didn't do you any justice.

Jen: Bitch.

Daz: Where now?

Jen: Macca's. I'm starving.

Scene 3

Sue: (*to audience*) Cue Daz's mum. Three sons, our Daz is the middle one. His older brother Paul left home and went to uni. Callum is twelve, and a pain in the rear. Getting Callum to have a wash is like trying to run the London Marathon backwards with your eyes shut. Mind you, our Darren would probably give it a go, always up for a challenge! He's never given us an ounce of trouble, our Darren . . . well, OK, we have had the odd incident, they all go through it . . .

Flashback to drunken vomiting. **Sue** *stands over* **Darren** *rubbing his back.*

Darren: (*in between vomiting*) Just another three inches . . .

Sue: Of what?

Darren: Pizza, an eleven inch . . .

Sue: You won't be told, will you? It's a good job your dad's not here. You've no right drinking at your age.

Darren: I didn't. It was the pizza. Got it from . . .

Both: . . . Roberto's! Well dodgy!

Sue: We should be suing that Roberto for the number of dodgy pizzas he's fed you! (*To audience*) It's the usual things that they all go through, but our Darren has always been fairly disciplined, he's into his football you see.

Both: My body is a temple.

Darren: I'm on a health and fitness regime. Coach reckons I've got potential.

Sue: So you won't be wanting my shepherd's pie then?

Darren: Go on then, need to keep my energy levels up . . . got any chunky chips to go with it?

Darren *exits.*

Sue: (*to audience*) He takes his training very seriously, always has. He dreams of being the next Beckham. Show me a young person who doesn't dream of being someone famous, of being someone else. Who am I to stand in the way of dreams?

Mac *enters.*

Mac:	(*to* Sue) Hiya love.
Sue:	Good day?
Mac:	Not bad, apart from the scratch on my car from our Callum's bloody bike again. Where is he?
Sue:	Shower.
All cast:	What?
Sue:	Yes. You heard right, it's his annual shower, dragged him in there kicking and screaming. (*To audience*) Our Callum's not into hygiene, he's going through a phase of ...
Callum:	(*shouts from offstage*) What? I'm using deodorant.
Sue:	But you haven't washed first, there's a few days of smell under there, deodorant doesn't disguise it.
Mac:	(*as though shouting upstairs*) Callum, when you've finished I want you down here!
Sue:	After you've rinsed the bath out, it'll need a good rinse after you've shed your muck.
Mac:	Where's our Darren?
Sue:	Training and then out with Jen.
Mac:	(*holds up some tickets*) Look what I managed to get hold of.
Sue:	Liverpool and Man U tickets! HHHow did you get them?
Mac:	I have my contacts. Can't wait to see his face.
Sue:	Did you get one for Callum?
Mac:	Yep, but he gets nothing until he explains the scratch.
Sue:	And cleans my bath.

Scene 4

All cast:	A teen's relationship with the mirror. When I look in the mirror I see ...

We hear a soundscape of things like 'spots', 'grease', 'stubby nose', 'small boobs', 'boobs', 'buck teeth', 'sex'.

The cast now become the football team and the changing room.

Mac:	A right unhealthy, pathetic rabble, a shower of ...
Darren:	(*as though he has just run in late*) Sorry I'm late Dad.

Mac:	No problem son. Arrive late looking knackered having spent all night on the park snogging the girlfriend, drinking and eating crap, all ready to perform to the very best of your ability …
Darren:	Give me a break.
Mac:	A break! That's exactly what I thought you were after son, a lucky break, you and the rest of this shower. What a joke! At this rate you'll be lucky to make it on the pitch, let alone score a goal.
All cast:	Pathetic, the lot of you!

The lads now begin to exercise, during which time the following conversation takes place.

Wayne:	(*to* Darren) You out last night Daz?
Darren:	Only with Jen.
Wayne:	Didn't get much sleep then?
Darren:	Leave it will you, she's not like that, your sister.
Wayne:	Glad to hear it.
Darren:	Eh, guess what? Dad got me tickets for the Liverpool–Man U game.
Mac:	Oi, you two! Get on with it! A shambles. What's got into you Darren? I can't hear you lads!
All lads:	No pies, exercise, No pies, tone those thighs, No pies, exercise, No pies, tone those thighs.
Mac:	(*taking* Darren *to one side*) You need to sort your act out lad, your my best player and at present you're not up to scratch.
Darren:	I know Dad, I'm sorry. I promise I'm going to sort myself out, get myself in shape. I won't let you down.

*Cast disperse and the scene shifts to **Darren's** bedroom. He is looking in the mirror, **Sue** creeps up behind him.*

Sue:	Well, don't we just look gorgeous.
Darren:	Mum!
Sue:	Caught you posing!
Darren:	No I wasn't!
Sue:	Checking your paunch.
Darren:	Do you reckon I've put weight on?
Sue:	It's in the genes, you've got it from your father.

Darren:	What?
Sue:	I'm only messing! Have you 'eck put weight on, there's nothing to you. If anything you need fattening up.
Darren:	No pies, exercise.
Both:	(*doing the exercise squats*) No pies, tone those thighs.
Sue:	(*laughing*) I'm trying, I'm trying! Enough of that, too much like hard work. Right, I'm off. Say hiya to Jen. (*Begins to leave, then turns back.*) Oh, by the way, there's a lasagne in the fridge if you want to warm it up before you go out.
Darren:	Why, where are you off to?
Sue:	Slimming World with Viv – and then probably out for a drink after to drown my sorrows. Had a chicken korma and three-quarters of a bottle of wine last night!

Sue *exits, leaving* Darren *gazing into the mirror.*

Darren:	(*whispering*) No pies, exercise.
Mac:	(*as if shouting from downstairs*) Darren, are you having some of this lasagne with me?
Darren:	Nah, I'll get something when I'm out.

Scene 5

All cast:	Scene change. The park.
All lads:	Out on the park mucking around, Sneak a little drink where we won't be found. Drink a bit of cider, have a little smoke, Be in by nine, what a bloody joke!
Wayne:	Alright Daz, where's Jen?
Darren:	Said she'd meet us in a bit, Kate's round there, think they're still getting ready.
Wayne:	Why does it take girls so long to get ready? Is it because they've got to apply six layers of make-up to hide the fact that they're so bloody ugly?
Darren:	Oi, my Jen's not ugly.
All lads:	She's gorgeous, phwooor!
Wayne:	Got any ale, Daz?
Darren:	Nah, my dad was in, couldn't get anything . . . anyway I'm not drinking.

© 2014, *Learning about Social Issues through Scripts for Learners aged 11–16*,
John Rainer and Kirsty Walters, Routledge

All lads: (*confused*) What?

Darren: I'm not drinking. I've got trials on Saturday, I've got to get fit.

All: (*taking the mickey*) No pies, exercise, no pies, tone those thighs, no chips, got wobbly bits, curry night, cellulite.

Darren: Funny.

Wayne: You are turning into one sad man, Daz.

Darren: No, it's just that ...

Darren, Jen and Sue: I've got dreams, nothing wrong with that.

> *The scene cross-cuts to **Jen**'s house where the girls are getting ready.*

Kate: Oh my God, how tiny are you?

A: Well tiny.

B: Now't there.

All: (*sigh*)

Jen: Me and Daz are on this healthy eating thing, you know, 'cos of his football and that. He's got to be dead disciplined now 'cos of his training.

B: He's dead serious about it then?

Jen: Yeah, well serious, I'm dead proud of him.

A: Fancy yourself as the next Colleen do you?

Jen: No she's well fat and ugly.

B: I've got a spot.

Jen: That's because of the bad toxins in your body.

> *Spotlight problem page.*

All: Dear Anne ...

A: My acne is getting worse, I don't think I'll ever get a boyfriend with skin like this.

All: Anne's reply ...

B: Wipe off the slap, cleanse those pores, swop the choc for a healthy lot. A healthy balanced diet is what's needed. Remember, you are what you eat, girls!

All: Bitch!

> *Spotlight off.*

A: Does my bum look alright?

Jen: A damn sight better than your face!

Scene 6

Sue: (*to audience*) It was the morning of his big match, we set off early to miss the traffic. We'd missed breakfast, called in at the drive-in McDonalds.

Mac: What you having Daz?

Daz: Nowt, not before the game, I can't play on a full greasy stomach, can I?

Sue: You've got plenty of time before the game Rooney. You can't play on an empty stomach either.

Daz: Leave it will you, I'm not eating that crap. I know what I'm doing.

Sue: (*to audience*) 'I know what I'm doing!' The number of times we heard him say that! He was so convincing, a sensible lad, we believed him. I believed him, I let it happen. You see, I believed he was in control. Young lads don't stop eating, do they? They just pick all day, grab something when they're hungry. Used to cost me a fortune in supermarket bills with all the rubbish he'd get through. Did I see him eat? Yeah … no … sometimes … you can't watch them 24/7, can you? I trusted him, believed he'd eaten when he said he had.

Jen: As the weight started to drop off I put it down to the extra training he'd been doing. Training most days …

Jen and Sue: Chasing his dream.

> *A football match is depicted in slow motion. We hear music/ commentary and see* **Daz** *scoring a goal, collecting the trophy, etc. The next piece of dialogue shatters this sequence.*

Mac: What the hell was that Daz? What is up with you lad? You were worse than useless out there, I'm taking you off, I'm subbing you. You're not taking this seriously son. Get some sleep, have a good think and come back to training in a few weeks. You can let me know then if you're serious about this, 'cos at the moment I really don't think you are. You're not just showing yourself up, son, you're showing me up as well …

Daz: Dad, please …

Mac: I mean it, Darren. You want to be a successful footballer, start taking it more seriously and stop wasting my time.

Daz:	(*to audience*) Who was I turning into? Why was I letting my dream slip away? I had every chance to achieve what I wanted, to be the best, but dad was right, I was worse than useless out there. Unfit, unhealthy, letting the team down . . .
All:	Letting your dad down.
Daz:	I knew what I had to do.
All:	(*whisper*) Pinch an inch, pinch an inch, no pies, exercise . . .

Scene turns into a conversation between **Daz** *and* **Jen**.

Jen:	Why haven't you phoned?
Daz:	I've been busy, got stuff on my mind.
Jen:	Stuff that's more important than me?
Daz:	Yeah . . . I mean no . . . it's just . . . Jen, you know how much my footie means to me, I've got to focus otherwise . . .
Jen:	Oh I get it, it's me that's the problem, is it? It's my fault that your dad's kicked you off the team . . .
Daz:	He hasn't kicked me off, he's just giving me time out to get myself sorted. I haven't been taking the training seriously enough, I've . . . it's all I've ever wanted to do Jen . . .
Jen:	And you don't want me distracting you.
Daz:	I don't need anything distracting me Jen. It's not that I want to finish or anything, it's just sometimes you . . .
Jen:	What? I what?
Daz:	You don't give me a minute, you're always . . .

Jen *turns to face* **Kate** *and continues a conversation with her.*

Jen:	In my face, it's like I can't breathe, he says. Then I started crying . . .
Kate:	They hate that, lads, crying.
Jen:	Yeah, well, I was upset. He just lost it, started going off on one, shouting at me . . .
Jen and Daz:	I can't deal with this now, I just need some space!
Kate:	And then what happened?
Jen:	I said, 'Fine!' and started walking out, then I turned back and said to him, 'You've changed Daz' . . .
Jen, Mac and Sue:	. . . And I don't like the person you're turning into.

Spotlight on **Kate** *as 'Agony Aunt'.*

Kate: Dear Anne, my boyfriend is becoming distant from me. Is it because he doesn't fancy me anymore?

Kate and Jen: Probably

All: (*whisper*) No pies, tone those thighs.

Jen: (*shouting at* Wayne) Get out of my room Wayne, this is a private conversation!

Wayne: Just checking if you were still crying. Just checking if it's possible to cry for eight hours non-stop.

Jen: Mum, tell him!

Helen: Wayne, leave her alone, she's upset.

Wayne: I just wanted to see how blotchy her face was now.

Helen: I said leave her. Go and get a wash, you stink! At least she can get a boyfriend, no girl's going to want to go anywhere near you with those pits.

Wayne: I like my smell, it's natural, sexy and very masculine. Not like Jen, she's just one big blotch.

Jen: Get out!

Wayne: (*making his way out*) Sorry to hear about you and Daz.

Jen: Why, what's he said ... has he said anything to you?

Wayne: No ... (*From offstage*) just that he doesn't fancy you anymore... (*Bobs his head back in.*) Only messing!

Jen: What if he doesn't fancy me anymore though?

Kate: Course he does Jen, he's mad about you.

Helen: It sounds like he's a bit stressed out love. Why don't you two get yourselves out and have a laugh, show him you aren't bothered. You can't stay up here forever love.

Jen: How can I go out, look at my face! And the point is mum, I am bothered.

Helen: Plenty more fish in the sea.

Jen: I hate fish, I've always hated fish!

Kate: It's very good for you actually, plenty of omega-3, good for your brain ... OK, we'll stay in. Do you want another chocolate?

Helen: You watch, he'll be texting any minute saying how sorry he is ...

Jen: I'm not letting him get away with it this time, he can't speak to me like that.

Text message goes off. **Jen** *springs to read it.*

Jen: It's Daz.

Jen and Daz: (*as though reading the text message*) Soz babe shouldn't ave had a go at u, sorted my head out luv you lots, meet me later (*sarcastically*) question mark.

Kate: Where are you going?

Jen: Where do you think? Meeting Daz, of course!

Helen: I thought you just said . . .

Jen: Help me get rid of my blotches!

Scene cuts to **Daz's** *house.*

Sue: Darren, your tea's ready.

Daz: I'm not hungry. I'm off out to meet Jen.

Sue: But you've not had anything to eat.

All: I'll get something when I'm out!

Jen and Daz: See you later mum!

Daz *and* **Jen** *face to face.*

Daz: Sorry.

Jen: Sorry.

Both: Forget it.

Helen: (*to audience*) And just like that, everything was OK again . . . for a while.

Scene 7

The scene opens in the changing room.

All: Some locker room advice from the sportsmen of tomorrow.

All cast become the lads in the changing room. The following sequence should be done with movements which depict getting dry and changed after a shower.

All: Biceps, triceps, try to get a six pack,
Sit ups, press ups, try to lose some more.
Biceps, triceps, cut the carbohydrates,
Bend it, stretch it, till every muscle's sore.

All point and laugh at one of the lads.

All:	Man boobs!

The above chant is repeated, but this time with backs to the audience. It ends with all peering down at one of the lads' 'private' parts.

Daz:	What is that?

All turn to audience and wiggle little fingers to reflect what they have just observed.

Wayne:	You coming for something to eat Daz? I'm starving.
Daz:	Nah, I'm watching my six pack.
Wayne:	My body is a temple and all that?
Daz:	Yep, I've got to keep in shape, got the England Schoolboys try-outs coming up, haven't I? I'm on a detox.
Wayne:	Sounds painful that. See you later.
Daz:	Yeah see you later mate.

Daz *admires his physique in the mirror.* **Mac** *approaches.*

Mac:	You're looking much better son, told you the hard work would pay off. Today Sunday league, tomorrow the premiership – trust me. Keep up the good work.
Daz:	(*to audience*) So I did, I kept up the good work . . . I cut the carbs again. I cut the fat, cut the portions and I felt great. I felt good about myself.

Steps onto imaginary scales and is clearly pleased with what he sees.

Daz:	Yes! Come on!
Sue:	(*to audience*) But a few weeks later there was a noticeable change in him. He was moody, not like my Darren. Weight kept dropping off, it was noticeable in his face. He always had an excuse ready for why he couldn't eat . . .

Different cast members represent **Darren's** *excuses.*

A:	I'll get something when I'm out.
B:	Feel a bit off.
C:	I've had something at Jen's, I'm not hungry.
D:	I've not got time.
Mac:	(*to audience*) He was becoming obsessed with his diet. When he hit one weight loss target, he set himself another.

Sue:	(*to* Daz) Darren, what have you eaten today?
Daz:	Loads. See you later, I'm off out.
Mac and Sue:	Training!
Mac:	(*to audience*) I blamed myself. Pushed him too hard, gave him the wrong messages. What kind of a father would do that to his son? But then, two weeks later . . .
Jen:	That's great news!
Daz:	(*to audience*) I was selected for the England Schoolboys team!
Mac:	(*to* Daz) I'm so proud of you son.
All:	This is serious stuff now.

Scene cuts to the park at night. The cast become the lads out for the night.

A:	Alright Daz? Not seen you for ages.
Daz:	Alright lads? I've been training loads at the moment, getting into shape.
Wayne:	Heard about your news mate, well done.
B:	What's that then?
All:	Selected for the England Schoolboys.
Wayne:	Remember us when you're rich and famous, won't you?
B:	And surrounded by gorgeous women.
Daz:	There's only one woman for me.

Jen appears in the background.

A:	Fancy a drink, Daz?
Daz:	Nah, got to watch myself now.
All:	No pies, exercise!
Daz:	No, it's just dead important that I . . .
Wayne:	Come on Daz, you're celebrating. Don't go all boring on us now, things are starting to get exciting.
Daz:	I suppose there's no harm in a couple.

During this sequence we see the lads drinking and **Daz** *becoming more intoxicated.*

Jen:	(*to audience*) One bottle of 'Stella' went straight to his head, so then he had another and another until . . .

The drinking gets out of hand. **Daz** *is unable to stand up straight.*

Wayne: He's wasted!

Jen: It's not funny Wayne, he's got training in the morning, he's not eaten anything, he's drinking on an empty stomach.

Wayne: Stop making excuses for the fact that he can't take his ale, Jen.

Jen: This is your fault Wayne, you should know better. (*To Daz*) Come on, let's get you home, you're bladdered.

Daz: (*very drunk*) Leave me alone, stop spoiling it, you're always spoiling things. I'm celebrating!

All: Cue the trouble!

Jen: (*to audience*) That's when these other lads approached. We knew of them, the types who were always out for trouble. One of them in particular was jealous of Daz.

Members of the cast represent the lads from the other 'gang'.

A: Looking good Darren, glad to see you're man enough to take your ale.

Jen: Leave him will you. He's celebrating, he's just been selected for the England Schoolboys, more than you'll ever do.

A: Ooh, calm down love, anyone would think you were a bit stressed out. Can't be easy going out with a pisshead though, can it?

Daz: What did you say?

A: You could do better than that Jen. I'll show you what it's like to be with a real man if you like. One who can take his ale.

Daz: Shut your mouth or I'll shut it for you.

A: I doubt it mate, you can't even see straight. Come on Jen, I'll show you a good time.

Daz: I said shut your mouth

Wayne: He said shut it.

A: Or what?

All cast represent the punch – perhaps by punching out and making the noise by slapping their chests.

Jen: (*to audience*) I can't even remember how it started, it happened so quick. He went mad, out of control, I'd never seen him like that before. He just went for him and when he was down, he just kept on kicking and kicking.

All cast represent the kicking by stamping in unison on the floor.

Jen: (*to* Daz) Leave him, Daz!

Wayne: Daz that's enough, leave him!

Jen: Daz, will you listen, please!

Sue: (*to audience*) The police brought him home. My son. I'd never seen him in a state like that before. He was totally out of it, covered in blood. The next day we tried to sit down and talk . . .

Daz, Sue and Mac: Calm, civilised . . .

Mac: Furious! No son of mine comes home to this house in a state like that.

Sue: Please love, don't start shouting, he's been punished enough.

Mac: I haven't even started yet. You give me the best news I could possibly ever have, that you've managed to get selected for the England Schoolboys, and then what do you do? You throw it all back in my face doing something like that. Being brought home like some thug, some drunken thug whose parents don't have a clue how to control him. The way the police looked at us, the shame. Well son, you really have proved your love and commitment to the game this time.

Daz: I do love it, I don't know what happened.

Mac: Well, I'll tell you what's going to happen now, shall I? You're grounded. No more socialising, no more Jen, no more training for a week, and certainly no Liverpool–Chelsea match.

Mac tears up the football tickets and throws them down in front of Daz.

Daz: Dad, you can't . . .

Mac: Just did. You let us down son.

All: Sort yourself out!

Sue: (*to audience*) So he did, he skipped three meals that day and then the next and then the next. (*To* Daz) Darling, you've got to eat . . .

Daz: I said I'm not hungry.

Cast simultaneously tear down football posters from the wall.

Sue: (*to audience*) There was no doubt in my mind that he'd got himself so drunk that night because he hadn't eaten anything. There wasn't enough food inside him to soak up the alcohol. It was a downwards spiral from that point. For the next few weeks he seemed to change before our very eyes. He became more obsessed with his weight and his diet. When Darren looked in the mirror he saw . . .

Daz and Sue: Fat. Useless. Pathetic.

Sue: Fat that he thought would stand in the way of his dream. There was no convincing him. (*To* Daz) You are not fat, Darren.

Jen, Mac and Sue: We should have seen it coming.

Scene 8

Sue: (*to audience*) During the time in which he had been grounded, Darren had sulked and pleaded with his dad to let him train but once my husband makes up his mind there's no budging him.

Mac: He's got to bloody learn, Sue!

Sue: (*to audience*) When he eventually started back at training he was visibly much weaker. The weight had dropped off even more, he was moody, tired, just not himself. No matter how much we tried to make him eat, he was determined that he knew what he was doing.

Daz: I'm not eating that, it's full of fat, I said I'll sort my own meals.

Sue: I thought that the only way to get through to him was to have a word with his coach. It was a Sunday training session when he took him to one side.

Wayne: (*as new coach*) You decided to turn up today then, grace us with your presence?

Daz: Sorry boss, I overslept.

Coach: Well, If I'd have been you today Daz, I'd have stayed in bed. You were worse than useless out there, lad.

Daz: I know, look I'm sorry, I'll get it sorted . . .

Coach: Your time keeping's appalling, you look absolutely knackered . . .

Daz: I've not been sleeping, that's all . . .

Coach: Your mum tells me that you've not been eating, either.

Daz: Oh, not this again, she's on my back all the time.

Coach: She's worried about you Darren, and so she should be. You're all skin and bone, lad.

Daz: I know what I'm doing, I just want to keep in shape, I want to get fit.

All: You're fit for nothing!

Coach:	You haven't got enough strength or energy to play as it is, if you lose any more weight there'll be no point you turning up to a game 'cos I'll be subbing you as soon as you start playing. You're ruining your chances Darren. I've got no choice but to do this. You're off the team until you've sorted yourself out. It's for your own good.
Daz:	One minute you're telling me to take things seriously and then the next you're punishing me for doing exactly that.
Coach:	You're taking things too far, Darren.
Daz:	(*To* Sue) This is your fault! Why couldn't you keep your nose out?
Sue:	(*to audience*) And just like that, his dreams were shattered and it was all my fault. When he looked in the mirror he no longer saw a premiership footballer, he saw . . .
All:	. . . A reflection he didn't like.
Daz:	Fat. Useless. Pathetic.
Jen:	Daz, what is wrong with you? Talk to me, please!
Daz:	Why can't you all just get out of my face and leave me alone? I just need some space.

To classical music we see a depiction of a football team in which **Daz** *scores the winning goal. It then turns sour as match tickets are torn up, hands go to stomachs – and then we see* **Daz** *slowly trying to put food into his mouth and then being unable to do so.*

Scene 9

The scene takes place in **Daz's** *bedroom.*

Wayne:	Daz, your mam's worried about you mate, she says you're starving yourself. Jen's dead worried too, I heard her talking to Kate.
Daz:	Talking about what? I'm doing this for her, getting into shape so I can get back on the team.
Wayne:	But mate, you're making yourself ill, there's nothing to you.
Daz:	What you trying to say, that I'm a wuss?
Wayne:	Course not . . .
Daz:	That I'm not strong enough to take you on anymore?
Wayne:	No . . .
Daz:	One strike and you're down . . .

Goes to strike **Wayne** *but flounders.*

Wayne:	You're punishing yourself mate.
Daz:	I know what I'm doing.
Wayne:	And you're punishing Jen, she doesn't know what she's done, why you won't see her.
Daz:	I've had stuff on, she's got to understand football comes first.
Wayne:	She's my sister Daz and I won't have you upsetting her.
Daz:	It's none of your business Wayne, now if you don't mind I've got stuff to do.
Wayne:	What's happened to you Daz? You've changed, you used to be sound. You're taking this fitness thing too far.
Daz:	Oh I get it, you're jealous.
Wayne:	What?
Daz:	You hate the fact that I'm getting somewhere with my football, that I'm doing better than you …
Wayne:	What you on about?
Daz:	Can't take it, can you?
Wayne:	I don't have to listen to this crap. Grow up, Daz.
Daz:	I have grown up, unlike some, I've got a future ahead of me and you can't stand it.

Wayne *begins to leave.*

Daz:	I know exactly what I'm doing.
Wayne:	(*to audience*) It's hard when your mate who you've grown up with suddenly becomes a stranger. He was turning into a different person, someone I didn't know or like. Looking after his appearance was something he'd always done, but now it was getting out of hand. The trouble was everyone could see it apart from him. There was just no talking to him.

Scene 10

Sue:	Darren, you have got to eat something.
Mac:	It's not right, what you're doing, son.
Jen:	Why won't you talk to me, Daz?
All:	(*whisper*) Pinch an inch (*x3*)

Cast surround **Daz** *and become the voices in his head.*

A:	Fruit
B:	Veg
C:	Steamed
D:	Fresh
A:	Portions
B:	Small
C:	Eat
D:	Heave
A:	Eat
B:	Reject
C:	Sweat
D:	Vomit
All:	Punish
A:	Eat
B:	Reject
B:	Sweat
D:	Vomit
All:	Eat!
Daz:	No! Just leave me alone.
All:	I know what I'm doing!
Sue:	(*to audience*) It went from being faddy, picky, to eating only certain foods. Steamed veg – and only small portions . . .
Daz:	(*to Sue*) . . . Which I will measure.
Sue:	(*to audience*) Then it became a total refusal to eat. It was like the food he had once loved had become the enemy. Eating was painful, like torture, and I was the one forcing him to do it. I got tired of pleading with him.
Daz:	I said I don't want it, leave me alone! You don't understand, mum!
Sue:	(*to audience*) I didn't understand. I thought it was only girls who got obsessed with their weight.
Mac:	(*to Daz*) Don't you talk to your mother like that. Sit down and eat.
Daz:	Why? So I can get fat, so I can be a disappointment again. It's your fault I got chucked off the team in the first place. Making me eat crap, making me fat.

Mac:	Watch your mouth. I said sit down and eat!

Mac: Watch your mouth. I said sit down and eat!

Sue: Leave him Mac, please!

Mac: How can I bloody leave him? He's wasting away. You're not right in the head lad!

Daz: Never right, am I? Can't do anything right.

Half the cast: Pinch an inch, pinch an inch.

Other half: Who am I to stand in the way of dreams?

A: When I look in the mirror I see ...

B: No pies, exercise.

All: I will not eat! (*x3*)

> *All cast move slowly closer to* **Daz** *until* **Mac** *raises his arm as though about to hit* **Daz**.

Mac: Eat!

Daz: Go on, hit me! If it makes you feel better, do it!

Sue: (*to audience*) As a dad, Mac felt he had failed his son. There was nothing wrong with our other two sons, so why was this happening to Darren? Why couldn't he sort it out?

Mac: (*to audience*) Why did I feel so helpless? When they're born, you hold them in your arms and you feel this overwhelming sense of responsibility for that little person. They stare back at you with those tiny, helpless, scared little eyes, scared of this unknown world they've just entered into. As you hold them in your arms, you think, whilst I'm your dad, you'll never need to be scared of anything, son. You'll never be scared of anything, I'll make sure of that ... I promise ...

Scene 11

Sue: You hear of these things happening to girls, eating disorders, but not with lads, do you? We couldn't believe what we were hearing when the doctor diagnosed Darren as suffering from ...

Dr Barker: Anorexia nervosa, Mrs Thomas. Darren has a very distorted view of his body.

All: (*whisper*) Fat. Useless. Pathetic.

Dr Barker: He is unable to think rationally about food. He is starving himself because he is unsatisfied with the way he looks. Food is the enemy to Darren.

Mac:	But he's practically skeletal.
Dr Barker:	Not in his mind. He sees it all very logically, he's convinced himself that what he's doing is right.
Sue:	But he's wasting away. My big, strong boy.
Dr Barker:	True, but when Darren looks in the mirror he sees something very different to what the rest of us see.
All:	The mirror tells a very different story.

A cast member represents the mirror. A series of mirror images between **Daz** *and the mirror take place before the mirror speaks.*

Mirror:	Darren, you've overindulged again, haven't you?
Daz:	You're right, I have. It's OK, I'll sort it.

Darren *picks up a plate and is seen counting peas onto the plate.*

Sue:	Darren, what are you doing?
Daz:	Counting. I've lost count now. I'll have to start again.
Sue:	(*to audience*) Every mouthful monitored, counted, checked.
Mac:	This is ridiculous, you can't go on like this, we can't go on like this.

Throughout the next argument, **Daz** *continues to count as though oblivious to what is going on around him.*

Sue:	Don't shout at him, Mac.
Mac:	Isn't it about time you stopped protecting him, Sue? It's no wonder he's the way he is. Too much pandering to him, pussyfooting around him.
Sue:	So now it's my fault he's like this, is it? Nothing to do with the amount of pressure you put him under with his bloody football.
Mac:	What are you saying?
Sue:	I'm just saying that if you hadn't bloody well pushed him all the time . . .
Mac:	Incredible, isn't it? My son's mental health problems are my fault now . . .
Sue:	Don't say that, he hasn't got mental health problems . . .
Mac:	There you go again woman, protecting him, it's about time we faced up to the truth, our son is ill . . .
Sue:	Just leave it Mac . . .

Mac:	(*exiting*) I can't take this anymore, is there nobody in this family who is living in the real world?
Sue:	(*to audience*) He was right, I didn't want to face the truth. (*To Daz*) Darren, love, please talk to me, look at me.

They look at each other for a few seconds. **Darren** *gets up and walks away.*

Sue:	(*to audience*) With anorexics, they don't realise how much they are hurting themselves and those closest to them. (*Shouting after* Daz) Jen phoned again love, she said your mobile was switched off again. She's upset, love. (*To* Jen) I think he just needs some time sweetheart, he's a very sick young man. Just give him some time.
Jen:	But I just want to be there for him.
All:	We all do.

Scene cuts to a conversation between **Helen, Kate** *and* **Jen.**

Jen:	He's lost so much weight, he just doesn't look like the same person anymore.
Helen:	What that woman must be going through, nobody knows.
Kate:	People have been asking questions at school.
Jen:	You haven't said anything, have you? We promised we wouldn't say anything. Daz wouldn't want people knowing.
Kate:	I said he got injured at football.
Jen:	What am I going to do, mum? I feel so useless.
Helen:	Just give him time love and remember it's not you, it's him.

Scene 12

Sue:	(*to audience*) The trouble with people with eating disorders is that they are in denial of their condition. They don't think they have a problem.
Daz:	There's nothing wrong with me, I don't need help!
Sue:	(*to audience*) The school were very supportive, as were the doctors and nurses who looked after him each time he was admitted to hospital.

A 'V' shape is formed by the cast. Each takes one of the following lines.

A:	How are things, Mrs Thomas? We're all thinking about you.
Sue:	We're anxious that the kids at school don't find out what's wrong with him, Darren would be very embarrassed.
B:	Anorexia, didn't think lads could get that.
C:	His mum wants it kept quiet.
Jen:	Who told you that? No, it's not true, he's just not well, done too much with the training and everything.
D:	It's my job to provide support for Darren and yourselves.
A:	Apparently he can hardly walk he's that weak.
B:	He got a place with the England Schoolboys, you know.
Jen:	Yeah, course we're still going out, I see him all the time.
C:	Fancy a kick about?
D:	His parents must be out of their minds.
A:	If there's anything we can do to help.
Sue:	(*as if trying to spoon-feed* Daz) You've got to help yourself love . . . please, one mouthful . . . for me. . .
Daz:	(*turning away*) I can't.
Mac:	There's no such word as 'can't', you're not bloody trying. I thought you wanted to make something of your life, I thought you had dreams.
Sue:	(*to audience*) But dreams were a thing of the past. No dreams anymore, just nightmares.
Mac and Sue:	Every day a living nightmare.
Mac:	(*shouting at* Daz) Just eat, will you? (*Almost inaudible*) Please son . . .

Daz *gets up as if moving away from the table.*

All:	Will not eat, will not eat, WILL NOT EAT!

Daz *collapses to the floor.* Mac *goes to pick him up.*

Mac:	(*to audience*) I carried him to bed that night. He was too weak to walk.
Sue:	(*to audience*) The next day he was admitted to hospital once again. A constant yo-yo back and forth from hospital. Every time he was discharged we faced another battle to get him to regain weight again. We weren't winning that battle. Family life torn apart. Our other sons almost forgotten in the midst of all our problems with Darren.

All:	You've got three sons, not one!
Sue:	Guilt, constant guilt.
Mac:	Month after month, relentless worry. He was discharged from hospital, re-admitted, discharged, re-admitted, until . . .
All:	Congratulations, Darren! You have reached your goal weight, six stone, six pounds!
Mac:	(*to audience*) He was wasting away, no strength left. My son, the lad who was once a fit, healthy, young footballer with a promising future was nothing but an empty shell. He was disappearing pound after pound, stone after stone.
All:	I didn't think things like that happened to lads.
Sue:	(*to audience*) I'd search the internet for information on boys with eating disorders, there was so little information on the subject, it said it all. As a society we think it's only girls who obsess about appearance and weight.
All:	Not lads!
Mac:	Food became the enemy and he had lost the strength to do battle with it.
All:	You are what you eat!
Daz:	But I eat nothing, therefore I am . . .
All:	(*whisper*) Nothing.

Daz curls into a ball almost like the foetal position. The cast form a 'V' shape around him.

A:	Fit, healthy.
Daz:	Heave.
B:	Funny, charming.
Daz:	Vomit.
C:	Kind, caring.
Daz:	I don't want to talk about it.
D:	Fit, athletic.
Daz:	I will not eat!
A:	You're throwing away your chances.
B:	Chew, swallow.
Daz:	I will not eat!

C: A great future ahead of you.

D: Swallow.

Daz: I will not eat, I will not eat, I will not eat!

All: (*whisper as Daz tries to get up but fails*) Pinch an inch, pinch an inch, pinch an inch.

Daz: Today, Sunday league – tomorrow, the premiership. I know what I'm doing.

Sue, Mac and Jen: Who are we to stand in the way of dreams?

Dr Barker: I'm sorry, Mrs Thomas, but he'll have to be admitted.

Daz: (*to* Sue) Please don't make me go back in there, please Mum!

Dr Barker: If he doesn't gain weight, Mrs Thomas, Darren will die.

Scene 13

Jen: (*to audience*) His final days in hospital were worse than any nightmare. His body had started to go into shutdown.

Wayne: (*to audience*) It was hard to recognise him. Daz, the lad who scored goals, hung out in the park on a Friday night. I almost didn't want to visit him in hospital because I wanted to remember him as he was, not like that.

Sue: (*to audience*) When our Darren smiled, his whole face would light up.

Jen: (*to audience*) The room would light up. He has always been the life and soul of the party, then suddenly the light went out. I remember one of the last conversations I had with him before he died. (*To* Daz) I love you.

Daz: No you don't, Jen, you pity me. I see it in your eyes. You feel you've got to stay with me 'cos I'm like this.

Jen: That's not true, I want to be with you.

Daz: You walk past a mirror, Jen, and you check what you look like twenty times a day. A little voice comes into your head and it casts doubt but you can ignore it because you're perfect.

Jen: But I never see perfection, very few people do.

All: I always find something wrong with myself.

Daz: That little voice popped into my head each time I looked in the mirror, but slowly it got louder and louder until I couldn't hear anything else. A voice constantly telling me I was . . .

All:	Fat. Pathetic. Useless.
Daz:	I used to like what I saw in the mirror, Jen, but that stopped and all I could see was my faults, a bit of weight that might stand in my way of becoming a top player.
Jen:	Why didn't you talk to me about it?
Daz:	You used to make me feel so good about myself, Jen, but now you make me feel small every time you look at me. Because I know you're looking for the person I once was – and you can't find him.
All:	He's gone.
Sue:	(*to audience*) It had gone too far. He just didn't have the strength to fight anymore. The final time he was admitted to hospital he weighed six and a half stone. He was just fading away before our very eyes.
Mac:	(*to Daz*) I've got two tickets for the Liverpool–Man City game, just for you and me when you get out, when you get better.
Sue:	(*to audience*) Blame is the easiest thing to do, blame yourself, punish yourself. Why couldn't we have done more to help him?
Mac:	(*to Sue*) He's got to help himself, love.
Sue and Mac:	(*to audience*) He was such a fit, healthy young lad.
All:	Living the dream.
Mac:	(*to audience*) I'll never understand.
Sue:	Name one young person who doesn't dream of being someone else.
Mac:	(*to audience*) I held him in my arms and watched him slowly slip away. (*To Daz*) I'll always be proud of you, son.
Daz:	(*to Mac*) I'm scared, Dad.
All:	(*whisper*) Night night, sweet dreams.
Sue:	(*to audience*) He died on 5 July at seven minutes past four. Funny how things stick in your mind – like exact details: seven minutes past. You never get over it, you know. When you lose a child it's the first thing you think about in a morning and the last thing on your mind at night. The pain never goes away. His room's just how he left it, a tip! The tickets for the Liverpool–Man City game are still behind the clock on the mantelpiece.

*The piece ends with a projection of a young **Daz** playing football. The images eventually merge into images reflecting body image issues and anorexia nervosa. As the film is shown the cast slowly disperse until the stage is empty, leaving only a football scarf centre stage.*

PATHWAY 1: KS3 – AN EXPLORATORY APPROACH FOR YOUNGER LEARNERS

This sequence of workshops enables learners to explore the play – the feelings of characters and the issues raised – through a variety of techniques, and in so doing gives learners opportunities to explore a sensitive area in safety.

Workshop 1: Understanding more about eating disorders and what might go on in the mind of a sufferer

Resources needed for this workshop

Magazines.

Chocolate and sweet wrappers.

Weighing scales.

Poem.

Images of celebrity icons, size-zero models, male suffering from anorexia/bulimia.

Music for performance piece.

Key facts about eating disorders.

Invite the learners to consider a pre-prepared *set-up*: chocolate bars, magazines, etc., and ask them to consider the symbolism of the props. How do they interpret the set-up? What words, phrases or questions does it evoke?

Now place a set of bathroom weighing scales in the arrangement and ask learners how this might have altered their response.

Show the group images of conventionally attractive celebrity icons and again ask learners to describe what they see. Now show an image of a 'size-zero' model, which should lead in to a discussion about eating disorders. At this stage we have found it helpful to introduce some facts about anorexia and bulimia. The final image shown should be of a male suffering from an eating disorder. Try to draw out of the discussion the learners' awareness of conditions like anorexia nervosa and more general social perceptions of eating disorders.

Arrange the learners in groups of three. One must take on the role of a person with an eating disorder and the other two must represent the two sides of the mirror, the 'angel' and the 'devil'. As a group, their task is to create three simple gestures or actions performed by the person looking into the mirror. These gestures are reflected by the other two people – who represent the mirror, and also the 'inner conscience' of the character. Once the gestures have been created,

Eating disorders

ask learners to consider what the two sides of the mirror might be saying to the sufferer; for example, *'It looks fine, you can't afford to lose any more weight'*, or *'That top is too tight, it's pulling, can't you see?'*

Watch and discuss some of the pieces.

Read the poem 'Eaten Away', which can be found at: http://www.caringonline. com/feelings/poetry/collection/eaten_away.htm.

Ask learners to consider how the 'inner mind' of the poet is revealed. Draw out key words, phrases and images.

Ask the learners to form groups of four or five and create a performance piece based on the poem entitled 'Inside the mind of an extreme dieter'. The group must choose three key images/moments and devise three group still images that effectively reflect them. Minimal movement can then be added to develop the piece. Words, sounds and phrases can also be added to reflect the 'inner mind'; music and lighting could be also be added to enhance the work.

Spotlight some of the pieces and ask learners to evaluate the effectiveness of each piece. What strategies were used to reflect the 'inner mind'? What were the strengths of the piece? 'A star and a wish' could be used here:

The bit that shone out was . . .

I wish that they had . . .

Plenary cards will assist learners' reflections on their work so far, and can be easily made on pieces of laminated card. Ask volunteers to choose from one of the five cards and share with the rest of the group:

- L – Something I learned this workshop
- * – A drama star/someone who stood out for good work this workshop
- S – A skill that has been used today
- ? – A question for the class based on the workshop
- T – A target for improvement next workshop for myself or someone else.

Extended learning

Research some facts about eating disorders, or find an article or image that could be shared next workshop.

Workshop 2: The play

To gain an understanding of the play *Waisted*, its characters, themes and issues.

> **Resources needed for this workshop**
>
> Copies of *Waisted* play script.
>
> Copy of Sue's monologue.
>
> 'Post-it' notes.
>
> Facts/statements about eating disorders for true/false starter.

Ask the learners to recap on work covered in the last workshop and share any research completed for homework. Give each student two 'post-it' notes on which they must write 'T' for true and 'F' for false, and read out a series of statements/facts about eating disorders. After each statement the learners must hold up the 'T' or 'F' depending on whether they believe it to be true of false.

The teacher, working in role as Sue, now gives brief background information relating to the story of her son, Darren. (Use the monologue provided below if necessary.)

> He was 16, had his whole life ahead of him. Dreamed of becoming a top footballer and, believe me, he was well on his way. I realise it's a mother's prerogative to boast, but my son really did have the talent. We never stood in his way, always encouraged and supported him. Perhaps that was the biggest mistake we made. You see, had we stood in his way a bit sooner, tried to make him see sense, we might just have saved him, might have stopped him before it got out of control. I can only hope now that our Darren's story can be used to help others, to stop another young person destroying their life too. If you're willing to listen, I'm willing to share. Here is Darren's story . . .

Read the play, stopping at key points to discuss and question. De Bono's *thinking hats* could be used here to give different perspectives on the issues raised.

Extended learning

Complete *learner's logs*.

Workshop 3: Darren and his motivation as a character

The aim of this workshop is to understand more about the character of Darren, and his motivation.

> **Resources needed for this workshop**
>
> Darren's 'most precious objects'.
>
> A cardboard box.
>
> Drawing paper and pens.

Start with a discussion of last workshop before re-introducing the character of Darren's mum (teacher in role): she produces a wooden box, opens it and looks inside. This is the box in which she keeps all of her most precious objects associated with Darren.

> In it I can see . . . photographs, toys, his first drawings . . . they all bring back a time in Darren's life – some happy, some not . . .

In order to model what comes next, select one object from the box – perhaps a toy – and talk about why it is significant: *I remember when his Dad bought him this . . .*

Working solo, ask each student to draw one object which mum might have placed in her box of precious objects. Once completed, ask some learners to talk about the object they have drawn and why it might be significant.

Building on this idea, introduce the idea of a photograph album of significant moments in Darren's life, with blank pages to be filled. In groups of four, ask the learners to create four still pictures – to represent photographs from different phases of Darren's life. Give each student the task of directing the other members of the group in constructing one image.

Once complete, ask the groups to consider ways in which the 'memory box' objects they previously drew might be incorporated into the images. Allow the learners to create a sequence of the four images, flowing from one to the next, and suggest that the final image in the sequence might signify what happens to Darren happens in the future: a turning point of some kind?

Before the groups present their work, suggest that the performed sequences might represent a flick through the family album; ask them to consider how they might represent how Darren alters as the years go by. Ask the group to try to relate this to their own lives.

Finally, ask groups to add captions to each of their images – the kind of thing mum might have written at the bottom of the photos in the album. If learners want to underline the meaning of their images even further, the spoken thoughts of characters might also be incorporated.

Allow rehearsal time, and share.

As a means of reflecting on the sequences, now ask each group to choose two contrasting moments in Darren's life to 'bring to life', paying attention to characterisation through acting techniques such as the use of voice, body language, spoken language and gesture, as they devise. In performance there should be a clear contrast shown between Darren's character in the early scene and the later one.

Allow time to evaluate the work.

Extended learning

Complete *learner's logs*.

Workshop 4: Exploring, creating and presenting a section of the *Waisted* script

> **Resources needed for this workshop**
>
> Copies of the *Waisted* play script (Scene 2).
>
> Pens and paper.

As a starter activity, ask the learners to use figurative mime ('body as props') to create group representations of the following:

- Football goalposts
- A trophy
- The ball
- A (working) white-line painting machine.

Distribute copies of the script and ask learners to focus on Scene 2 – the 'shop rails' scene.

Ask them to consider the possible ways in which the scene might be staged. What problems do they foresee? What will they need to do in order to begin to stage the scene?

Distribute pens and paper and ask each group to record – in the form of a spider diagram – the various questions or problems they will need to resolve in order to complete the task of staging the scene.

Now give each group a short section of the scene to work with and ask them to 'walk through' the scene, in order to get a basic sense of the physical layout and spatial relationships.

After some working time, ask groups to stage their section of the script – again with no dialogue – but paying particular attention to movement, space, facial expression, body language and proxemics.

Eating disorders

Now allow them to add in the dialogue, and run through the scene a couple of times.

Now ask the learners to experiment with performing the scene:

- at different paces,
- using different settings/spaces,
- driven by different emotions, for example tense, secretive, nervous, etc.

Learners can now create an extension to the scene they have been exploring by adding their own script and stage directions. The finished scripts should then be swapped with another group to rehearse and present.

As a plenary activity, ask the learners to consider what insight they gained from treating the scene in this way, in particular, beginning their exploration by concentrating on the physical relationships, without words.

What effect did altering the pace, spatial configuration and emotional 'temperature' of the scene have?

Extended learning

Complete *learner's logs*.

Workshop 5: Using specific drama techniques to devise a piece of drama – 'Dreams vs. Reality'

Resources needed for this workshop

Key drama strategies on small pieces of paper, folded into a box or hat:

Slow motion	*Pace*	*Movement*	*Gesture*
Chanting	*Still image*	*Choral speech*	*Soundscape*
Echoing	*Use of levels*	*Spoken thoughts*	*Symbolism*

'Success Criteria' A3 sheets.

Music to create appropriate atmosphere.

In two teams, learners take it in turns to take a piece of paper from the hat and describe, in words, the meaning of what is written. Each team gets 60 seconds to guess as many as possible. Points are awarded for each correct answer. This is a useful opportunity for learners to explore key terms that they will encounter during the workshop – in a fun, competitive way.

Based on the starter, in small groups, learners are now asked to create a 'menu' for non-naturalistic drama: a table or list of drama forms and techniques that could be used to structure a non-naturalistic piece. Able learners may well be able to add to the original list of terms.

Read the speech from the play in Scene 2: *Who am I to stand in the way of dreams?*

Ask learners to consider its meaning. For learners that are more able, introduce the notion of *irony,* and try to help them understand why this statement is ironic. Ask the learners to consider how Darren's dreams may differ from the reality of his life.

In groups of four or five, ask learners to devise their own non-naturalistic performance piece based on what they know of Darren's story entitled 'Dreams vs. Reality'. Remind learners of the menu of strategies that might be appropriate for this task.

It will be helpful to provide success criteria. For example:

Someone who is successful in this task will:

- Focus at all times
- Contribute ideas
- Communicate effectively with their group and the audience
- Devise an entertaining and original piece of drama
- Use a variety of non-naturalistic strategies
- Take on a key role within the piece and sustain it
- Perform with conviction and control.

Watch and evaluate the pieces using the success criteria as a prompt for feedback.

Extended learning

Set learners the task of creating a written account or storyboard charting the development of the piece and the group's choice of drama strategies.

Workshop 6: Opening up the play

Resources needed for this workshop

Graphic organiser sheet.

Pens and paper.

As a recap on prior learning, ask individual learners to jot down three questions about the play – or the work that they have explored so far – that they would like resolved.

As a class, ask learners to share their questions and take answers or suggestions from their peers. The intention here is open up the play and empower other learners to become 'mini-teachers' who may be able to provide 'answers' to the questions identified.

To encourage the learners to take ownership of the process, they will now take on the role of the playwright. Their job is to consider 'unseen characters' in the play – characters who don't actually appear in the play, but who may have been important in Darren's life.

In pairs, ask learners to complete the *graphic organiser* based around the three key characters in the play: Darren, his mum and his girlfriend. The task is to create a web of other characters who may be linked in some way to these three; for example, Darren may be linked to other team mates, a form teacher and someone he met in hospital.

Once they have a number of possible 'unseen' characters to work with, their task is to select one character who they think might be interesting to develop further, and address the following questions (presented on the back of the *graphic organiser* sheet).

Create a scene between the 'key character' and the minor character they have now created.

Share and evaluate.

Extended learning

Complete *learner's logs*.

PATHWAY 2: KS4 – A PERFORMANCE-SKILLS APPROACH FOR OLDER LEARNERS

Workshop 1: Page to stage – capturing and presenting inner thoughts

---

Resources needed for this workshop

Paper and pens.

Sections of *Waisted* play script (Scene 10).

Building blocks

Begin with a selection of vocal warm-ups, as the start of this workshop looks at the *vocal toolkit*. Possible suggestions are tongue twisters, or articulating the five vowels.

- Ask learners to consider the idea of a *vocal toolkit* and what it would consist of. This could be jotted down in groups in the form of a spider diagram and then shared with others until all ideas are pooled together. Headings to be identified are *pace, tone, pitch, volume, accent, rhythm.*
- Groups of five or six are now given the section of script from Scene 10, and are asked to consider how the performance of the scene could be enhanced using the vocal toolkit. Their first task is to experiment with ways of speaking the scene using as many vocal techniques as possible – almost as if for a radio play or when creating a *soundscape.*
- Groups now perform their work, whilst other groups mark on their spider diagrams any vocal techniques used as they listen. Evaluative feedback may be given after one or two pieces.

The challenge

Learners are now asked to develop their scenes by adding in movement, mime and gesture in order to depict what might be going on inside Darren's head.

Top tips/Ask the expert

Ask groups to perform the ongoing work for each other. What targets for improvement can they suggest?

Re-focus and refine

Pose the questions, 'What if there was another scene in the play where a character's inner thoughts, nightmares or demons could be revealed? Who might that character be? What strategies or techniques could be used in the creation of this scene?'

Learners have the opportunity to rehearse and present their newly created scenes.

Extended learning

Complete *learner's logs*.

Workshop 2: Performance support – technical aspects that can enhance performance

Resources needed for this workshop

Copies of *Waisted* play script.

Pens and paper.

Stage lanterns on stands (if possible).

Building blocks

Begin by discussing the different technical aspects of theatrical performance. How can meaning be created through 'performance support'?

Learners are now asked to focus upon how meaning can be created through lighting. Start by outlining technical terms such *spotlight, gobo, strobe, setting, transition, mood.*

Groups of three or four are asked to read a section of script (all groups are to be given the same section at this stage). Give ten minutes to consider how colour could be used in the scene, either symbolically or to create mood and atmosphere. Their task is to annotate the section of script with their lighting ideas.

After ten minutes, one spokesperson from the group must report to the rest of the class. (An alternative way to do this is for the spokesperson from each group to rotate around the other groups in order to feed back ideas.)

The challenge

Working in the same group as the previous task, learners are now asked to choose their own section from the play to light. Their task is to design the lighting for this section, and therefore they will need to annotate their script to indicate how they might use lighting to enhance meaning. They must also be prepared to 'pitch' (share) their idea to another group, perhaps by electing a team of 'mini-teachers'/'producers' whose job it is to go around and listen in on the design process and discussions and advise. This team could then become the 'producers' who are looking for the right lighting team to light their show.

Top tips/Ask the expert

During this stage in the workshop each group pitches/shares their ideas with the class (or the team of mini-teachers/producers). A decision can be made at the end of this exercise as to which of the lighting designs would work best, and thus ultimately be employed and used in the production.

Re-focus and refine

Learners are now told that the director of *Waisted* would like each team to incorporate another aspect of performance technical support into the chosen scene. Each group is now given an opportunity to choose either sound, music or projected images, and to consider how their scene could be enhanced with this aspect of technical design.

Groups may like to share their ideas.

There is opportunity for this workshop to be expanded and developed further should you wish to do so. Portfolios of design and evidence of the design process could be incorporated into the *challenge* section. Learners could take responsibility for one key aspect of performance support and be given the opportunity to experiment practically with their ideas.

Workshop 3: The duologue – an insight into the relationship between two key characters

> **Resources needed for this workshop**
>
> Pens and paper.
>
> *Prompt/Advice* cards.

Building blocks

Discuss what is meant by the term *duologue*.

Ask learners to turn to the person next to them and jot down on two separate pieces of paper two characters from the play. They then place the names face down in the centre of the circle/stage space.

Eating disorders

In pairs, learners come into the centre of the space and take one character name each; they must speak the thoughts of the character they have chosen, and it is the task of the audience to guess who they are. It may be interesting if both actors pick up the same character name but reveal very different aspects of the character through their spoken thoughts.

After a few pairs have completed this task, ask the group to consider which pairing was the most interesting, and why. Which could have been developed further, and how?

The challenge

In pairs, learners must devise their own *duologue* between two characters of their choice. The duologue should provide a greater insight into the feelings and relationship between the two characters. They may decide to choose one key character and a more peripheral character. Once chosen, they must begin the challenge by writing their individual monologue, and then consider ways of putting the two together to create the duologue.

Top tips

Ask each pair to join up with another pair – who will become their learning partners – and present the work created so far to each other. During the performances the pair who are observing use prompt cards to draw the performers' attention to details they may need to emphasise: *More expression required, slow down, add gesture, eye contact required, pause*, etc.

Re-focus and refine

Encourage the groups to consider ways of linking their two monologues to create interesting duologues; for example, by using *cross-cutting* techniques, incorporating moments of interaction between the characters, or adding in movement, mime and gesture. Allow time for this development to take place and if necessary ask learners to link up once again with their learning partners in order to gain more feedback and advice.

Learners may wish to present their duologues to a wider audience or film their pieces in order to self-assess and further refine their work.

Workshop 4: The theatrical trailer – capturing the essence of the play

Resources needed for this workshop

Clip of feature film trailer.

Building blocks

Begin by showing the group an example of a *film trailer* and discussing its key features. For example, you may wish to point out its key moments, techniques used to engage the audience or create suspense, or the use of narrative commentary.

Ask learners to consider what the play *Waisted* is 'about'. What is meant by the term *eating disorders*? How is the impact of such a condition shown in the play? How does the play chart the progress of Darren's disorder?

In groups, ask learners to create a two-minute 'speed run' version of the play. They must capture key moments and find economical ways to portray the progress of Darren's illness. Work can be shared, and evaluated.

The challenge

In groups of five or six, learners must create a theatrical trailer for the play *Waisted*. The trailer might incorporate some or all of the following elements: an engaging opening, key moments, narrative commentary, moments of suspense.

Top tips

Learners are asked to nominate one person from their group to now step out of the piece and watch is as a director. Their task is to stop the action at any point and adjust it as they see fit.

Re-focus and refine

Explain to learners that a technical fault now means that the groups cannot rely on sound to carry the meaning of the piece and to engage an audience. They must now consider how the trailer can be adapted using non-verbal techniques; for example, physical theatre.

After learners have rehearsed the second version of their trailer, ask them to choose which version (verbal or non-verbal) they would like to present to the audience. Their chosen piece can be shared and evaluated through a written evaluation of both pieces comparing their effectiveness.

Workshop 5: TIE – the Theatre in Education project

Resources needed for this workshop

Opportunities to research TIE.

Building blocks

Ask learners what is meant by TIE (Theatre in Education).

Give groups a research task to find out key information about a TIE company local to them. Key questions are:

- What is the company name?
- How many people are involved in the company?
- What types of productions do they perform?
- Who are their main audience?
- Where are they based, and what area do they serve?

Ask learners to present their findings to the rest of the class. Alternatively, you could give each group the key facts relating to a particular company, which they must organise into a presentation.

Allow groups to share their findings with the class.

Now explain to learners that they are going to form a TIE company of their own, and therefore must decide on a name (and slogan?), and allocate key roles amongst the group: actors, director, writers, etc.

The challenge

Explain to learners that they have been commissioned to devise and perform a short piece of theatre in education based on the issue of eating disorders, and inspired by ideas from the play *Waisted*. The piece is to be performed to a Key Stage 3 audience – learners aged 11–14 years.

Top tips

After some working time, groups are asked to 'pitch' or 'sell' their ideas to another group, who must provide feedback.

Re-focus and refine

Ask learners to use the feedback given in order to begin developing their piece. Learners could also choose to take a *change of direction* challenge, which provides an opportunity to redirect their ideas; for example, in adapting the piece for a younger, Key Stage 2 audience.

There is plenty of opportunity for this single workshop to be developed into a full performance project, and open up community links so that work produced can be performed to an audience outside of school.

Workshop 6: A practitioner perspective – links with Brecht

> **Resources needed for this workshop**
>
> Opportunities to research the theatre of Bertolt Brecht.

Building blocks

Ask the learners to consider the staging of the play and, in particular, the actors' relationship with the audience. For instance, what do they notice about the first scene in the play, and indeed Daz's first words?

At various points in the scene different characters, solo and in unison, speak directly to the audience, sometimes as the character, and sometimes (as in Daz's first words) as a narrator.

- What might be the theatrical effect of 'direct address' like this?
- If you were sitting in the audience, what might this make you think, or feel?

The challenge

One feature of the theatre of Bertolt Brecht (1898–1956) was its 'self-consciousness': Brecht deliberately framed many of his plays as stories or 'parables', which the cast enacted for the audience – in contrast, of course, to the conventions of naturalistic drama.

An example of this is *The Caucasian Chalk Circle*, which uses a *framing device* to show that the story of Grusha and Azdac is being enacted by the members of a collective farm in order to help resolve a land dispute.

In *Waisted* (besides direct address) how might the group emphasise the story-telling aspect of the style of the play?

In groups of five or six, can they stage the first section of the play and:

- Create a framing device that shows that the actors had 'come to life' from the pages of a football comic book?
- Create a framing device that shows the story of Daz is being re-enacted by a self-help group who have come together to support their own eating disorders?
- Create a framing device of their own, which again emphasizes the non-naturalistic aspects of the play?

Top tips/Ask the expert

After allowing some working time, ask each group to join with another and perform 'work in progress'. Encourage each group to give structured feedback.

Refocus and refine

Groups now continue to re-work their pieces before presenting them to the whole group.

In order to consolidate and extend learning, ask the class to research something about the work of Bertolt Brecht:

- His major plays
- His theory of alienation (*Verfremdung*)
- His social and political context
- The rise of Nazism in 1933 and its effects on German culture – and Brecht's life and work.

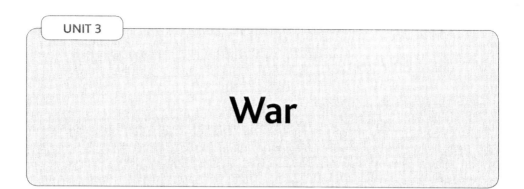

War

Introduction and context

The characters in *Lest We Forget* are all affected in some way by direct or indirect experience of the war fought by the UK, US and their allies in Afghanistan. During this conflict 444 members of the UK military died since 2001, with an estimated 24,000+ Afghan civilian casualties.

Approximately 20,000 people leave the UK armed services every year and the majority of them make the transition back into civilian life successfully. However, for some, life after front line action is not easy. Charities estimate that 4 per cent will suffer from post-traumatic stress disorder (PTSD), with a further 20 per cent likely to develop other mental health conditions; more soldiers and army veterans committed suicide in 2012 than were actually killed fighting the Taliban in Afghanistan. The charity *Homes 4 Heroes* estimate that 4,500 homeless ex-service personnel sleep rough in the UK.

Soldiers may also find the transition to civilian life difficult due to their lack of experience of work, and their levels of education. In the UK, more than one in four (28 per cent) of Army recruits were under the age of 18 when they joined up, and many have very low levels of literacy and numeracy.

The British armed forces have traditionally drawn non-officer recruits from young people with low educational attainment, often from disadvantaged back-grounds in areas of the country with high unemployment. Infantry recruits need only the literacy skills of a 5-year-old to join, and almost 40 per cent of Army recruits have the reading age of an 11-year-old.

Lest We Forget – The play

A note from the playwright

This play evolved as a result of the intense media coverage of the war in Afghanistan, and in particular footage of soldiers on their return to the UK. The play was written in response to a family member's involvement in the armed forces at the time, and was developed in consultation with him. It was first written and performed as a GCSE examination piece and was later developed into schemes of work for Key Stages 3 and 4.

There is opportunity for this play to become a wider school and community project: my school decided to use the play as part of an awareness-raising evening for the charity 'Help For Heroes'. We invited various organisations, including the local British Legion and representatives from the local 'Help For Heroes' branch, and produced a performance evening, which raised awareness and funds. Alongside the performance of the play, other departments across the curriculum took part, making it a whole-school event.

I have always found music from 'Spirit of the Glen' particularly effective in the performance of this piece.

KW

Lest We Forget

Kirsty Walters

Cast

Joe:	Young soldier traumatised by experience in Afghanistan
Amy:	Joe's mum
Peter:	Joe's younger brother
Brad:	Captain who loses his life in Afghanistan
Emma:	Brad's girlfriend
Elliott:	Soldier disfigured in Afghanistan
Meg:	Elliott's wife
Ash:	Soldier living on the streets

Scene 1

Scene opens with voice-over of news report on soldiers returning from Afghanistan. We see soldiers standing upstage in a line, facing front. All soldiers step down at the same time then march forward 'left, right, left', then sharp turn either left or right, leaving Joe *centre stage. He looks around, bewildered.* Amy *steps into the frame (cast disperse),* Joe *turns towards her.*

Joe: Hiya, mam.

Amy: Welcome home son.

Blackout.

Teacher: The trouble is, Mrs Nicholls, Joe cannot seem to help himself, he needs to . . .

Amy & Teacher: Control his temper.

Amy: Tell me about it. It can be over the simplest of things but usually it's when . . .

Teacher: . . . You tell him to do something.

All: Can't take orders!

Joe: Watch me. (*To audience*) I look back on who I was then, and it's hard to believe I'm the same person. Never the sharpest tool at school – teachers always on my back . . .

A: Try harder, Joseph!

B:	You're late!
C:	Concentrate!
D:	You'll walk out of those doors at the end of Year 11 with ...
Amy:	Nothing, no qualifications, no ambition, no future, Joe, if you don't sort yourself out.
Joe:	(*to audience*) It was like I had this deep-rooted anger, a chip on my shoulder, found it hard to be nice, do the right thing ... (*To* Peter) Get out my room!
Peter:	Mum says tea's ready.
Joe:	Don't want anything, I'm off out ... move! (*To audience*) If I wasn't larking around at school I was out ...
Amy:	(*as if on phone*) Fighting again ... what have you got to say for yourself?
Joe:	Now't ... see you later.
Amy:	I'm trying to talk to you.
Joe:	I don't want to talk ... (*To audience*) I was crap at most things, but one thing I was good at was using my fists ...
All:	Floored him, down in one!
Peter:	My brother, that, my hero.
Amy:	It's nothing to be proud of. You can't keep getting into trouble, Joe, I've got enough on my plate without constantly worrying about you. Your brother looks up to you, you're ...
All:	The man of the house.
Amy:	Can't you be a good example?
Joe:	(*to audience*) I guess one day something just clicked. I was bored of the same mates, the same fights, same thing night after night ...
Mate:	You coming out, Joe?
Joe:	Now't else to do, is there?
All:	School talk, careers ...
Joe:	The army were in ...
All:	It's certainly no easy career choice and definitely not for everyone ...
Amy:	Not for our Joe.
Joe:	(*to army guy*) S'cuse me, can I have a word? (*To audience*) They told me to join the local cadets ... finally I'd found something I loved.

Amy & Peter: You? In the army?!

Joe: Watch me.

All: My calling, my purpose ...

Lads: To fight for queen and country.

Joe: I chose a career in the army.

All: It'll be the making of you.

> *We see a training session taking place. Stylised movements and choral speech needed.*

> Biceps, triceps, got to get it right sir,
> Push-ups, sit-ups, can't stop now.
> Team tasks, killer tasks, trekking through the night tasks,
> Fighting for our lives tasks ... can't stop now.

Brad: What you slowing down for, Nicholls? Move it lad!

Joe: (*as if on phone*) I can't do it, mam, sick of being ordered around.

Mum: Come on love, don't give up. Don't forget, they're trying to break you.

All: Into tiny little pieces ...

Joe: Then build you back up again.

Ash: Into the bionic man, the machine, the robot.

All: And when they were up they were up, and when they were down they were down, and when they were only half way up ...

Joe: I don't know what I'm doing anymore.

Brad: Oi, Nicholls, get a move on. You're pathetic, what's up with you lad? You pining for your mummy?

Joe: No Sir.

Brad: Pardon?

Joe: (*a bit louder*) No Sir.

Brad: Pardon?

Joe: (*louder*) No Sir! (*To audience*) Just want to make them proud.

All: Make your country proud. Left, right, left ...

Brad: (*to* Emma) Right then, just about ready.

Emma: You got everything you need?

Brad: Yeah, sorted ... what's that look for? Come on love, you've done it before, you've managed, you've got through.

Emma:	I know, I just hate it when you're away, it's so difficult.
Brad:	Be back by Christmas. We'll have the most amazing time, I promise ... come on, show us that smile, something to remember.
All:	When we're apart ...

Quick flash to soldiers in Afghanistan – very fast-paced dialogue here.

A:	Stay close.
B:	Heads down.
C:	In position.
A:	No one gets left behind.
B:	It's what you do right now that makes a difference.
D:	Take aim!
Joe:	Breaking you down into little pieces.
Ash:	Bionic man, machine, robot ...
Brad:	Nicholls, move!

Lads freeze in image of war, **Brad** *steps out.*

Emma:	I love you.
Brad:	Love you too. I'll email ...
All girls:	I'll send the parcels, the letters, things to keep you going.
Lads:	To motivate, to spur us on.
Brad:	See you at Christmas, be the best yet, I promise.
Emma:	(*to herself*) Might get a ring!
All girls:	We pray ...
Meg:	We send them off.
Amy:	Wave goodbye to the boys ...
Amy & Meg:	And wait for them to return as men.
Emma:	If they are to return at all.

Scene 2

| All: | Touch down. Helmand Province. |
| Brad: | We've trained for this for years, for some of you it's your first time. Your friends and family back home are rooting for you. This is six months of your lives that could change the lives of the Afghan people |

forever. We're now a family, we've trained together, played together and now it's time to go on operations together. We are one unit, one family now. (*To audience*) As an officer you always put the men beneath you before you. Their welfare, their families back home, everything must come before you.

Ash:	(*to* Joe) Oi, baby face, move!
Joe:	What's his problem?
Elliott:	Your first time?
Joe:	Active service? Yeah.
Elliott:	Is it what you expected?
Joe:	Don't know what I expected, guess you're never really prepared.
Elliot:	True. Bit different to your training, eh?

Quick flashback to lads, raucous, taking part in a drinking game/chant. [Possible chant is: To the left, to the right, get it down you Zulu warrior, chug, chug, chug!] All duck down when Brad says . . .

Brad:	(*shouting*) Get down, we're under attack!
All lads:	Not a game anymore. The real thing.
Elliott:	How old are you?
Joe:	18 . . .
Ash:	Still wet behind the ears!
Elliott:	You'll be alright.
Ash:	Missing your girlfriend, are you?
Joe:	Nah, not got one.
Ash:	Best way.
Elliott:	Still living at home?
Joe:	Yeah, with me mam and me brother. He's thinking of signing up too, does everything I do.
Peter:	(*from background*) My brother, that, my hero.
Elliott:	Bet they're dead proud!
All girls:	His photo's up there above the mantelpiece.
Joe:	You two both married?
Ash:	Na, no way. Left no-one behind, no-one waiting when I get back, and that's the way I want it. This is my life, the army.

Joe: (*to* Elliott) What about you?

Elliott: Yeah, left the missus four and a half months pregnant. Should get home for the birth.

Cuts to **Meg** *with nurse at 20 week scan.*

Nurse: Everything looks absolutely fine. Do you want to know what you're having today?

Meg: Can you tell? Yeah I do.

Nurse: It's a little boy!

Meg: He'll be so thrilled, a son. (*To* Nurse) My husband's away in Afghanistan, he's in the army.

Lads: (*crouch down in firing position*) Helmand Province.

Cut to lads.

Joe: (*to* Elliott) Do you know what you're having?

Elliott & Meg: (*as though reading letter*) A son!

Elliott: I'm having a son!

Meg: (*to audience*) You get used to it. Being left behind, it's his job. It's not easy, though. All those exciting things he's missing. The scans, the first time I feel it kick, painting the nursery . . .

Girls: You, don't be overdoing it!

Meg: I won't . . . got to get things ready though, can't sit around and wait, there's things to be done . . .

All girls: While he's gone . . .

Emma: It's the little things you miss. Coming home from work after a bad day and not being able to tell him all about it, not feeling that security as he wraps his arms around you and tells you it'll be alright. You miss not being able to share a joke, you even miss the piles of clothes he dumps on the floor which he cannot seem to place in the laundry basket . . .

All girls: The way he always leaves the toilet seat up!

Emma: We were made for each other. He's the one, mum, I know he is.

Amy: The quiet . . . it's so quiet when he's away. Of course there's always our Kalen to keep me on my toes, but I miss him. Don't get me wrong, our Joe's always been a handful, but he's my eldest. There's always a special place for your firstborn, isn't there? There'll always be a place for you here son, this will always be your home.

Joe:	(*as though on phone*) Don't know if I can hack it, mam.
Amy:	Then come home, son.
Joe:	It's not as easy as that mam.
All girls:	We wave them goodbye and we wait ...
Brad:	See you at Christmas.
All:	We pray ...

> *'Spirit of the Glen' plays as we see lads in action. This scene should be done through movement, mime and gesture. In this scene we see* **Brad** *get killed. This could be done symbolically by simply having* **Brad** *rise and walk slowly back with arms raised in crucifix position. Two of the girls could hold the Union flag behind him as he walks to the back of the stage. The scene ends with* **Joe** *alone, sat down, traumatised.*

Scene 3

Joe:	(*rocks back and forth, almost inaudible*) He was ... I was ... I couldn't ...
Amy:	(*as though knocking on bedroom door*) Joe, please let me in. (*To* Peter) He just won't let me in.
Peter:	Mam, just leave him. If he doesn't want to talk, he doesn't want to talk.
Amy:	How can I just leave him? He's been in there for days, he's not been right since he got back home.
Peter:	I'll try again. (*He knocks*) Joe, it's me, can I come in? Think I've left some stuff in your room. Do you want me to break the door down?
Joe:	(*opens door*) Hurry up.
Peter:	You OK? You've hardly said a word since you got back ... mam's dead worried about you.
Joe:	No need, I'm fine ... Hurry up, will you?
Peter:	Got my application form, wondered if you'd read it over. I've started it but seeing as you've done it before thought you could help me.
Joe:	Did you?
Peter:	Yeah.
Joe:	Why do you want to join the army, Peter? I mean, I'd really love to know ... it's not a game, you know. Not just another little whim or hobby that Peter can have a go at then give up like he's done with everything else ...

Peter:	What you on about?

Peter: What you on about?

Joe: What was it? Oh yeah, karate, then the guitar, and then there was that time you fancied fishing, you got mam to buy all that fishing stuff, all the best gear, it had to be the best, everything you wanted you got, like a spoilt brat . . .

Peter: What is it with you, eh? Why can't you just give me a break? Why do you hate me so much, Joe, what did I ever do? I only wanted to see if you were OK, if you wanted to talk . . .

Joe: Talk about what? Talk about what, Peter? Why is it you and mam seem to think that I'll want to talk all of a sudden? We've never talked, we've lived under the same roof like strangers all these years, why would we want to talk now, eh?

Peter: We just want to help, try to understand.

Joe: Understand? OK, well understand this . . .

All other lads raise heads and come to life.

Elliott: We were under attack.

Brad: Don't go back out there without me.

Ash: We've got men back there . . .

Joe: Bullets, shells, the sounds . . . deafening . . .

Brad: Stay focused . . . I'll cover.

Elliott: Give me 90 degrees to the left . . .

Ash: (*to* Joe) You ever shot anyone before?

Joe: No.

Brad: (*shouting*) Why aren't you shooting?

Elliott: I'm in contact . . . Moving fast, dodging bullets . . .

Ash: Enemy . . . aim, fire, more ammunition needed, adrenalin pumping . . . take aim . . . this is what I trained to do . . . Contact report . . .

Elliott: Wait out.

Joe: Can't move, just frozen.

Brad: Why aren't you shooting?

All: Man down!

Elliott: The pain, sudden, excruciating, burning flesh . . .

Ash: He's been hit . . .

Brad:	Don't go back there without me … wait for my signal … Put those beneath you before you …
Emma:	Why? Why? Why you? Let someone else be the sacrifice …
Amy:	That's my lad out there …
All girls:	Turn on the news … can't watch, my lad's out there …
Meg:	(*on phone*) Hello, yes it's Mrs Mills here …
All girls:	Is it my lad?
Joe:	Can't move, just frozen, can't move …
Ash:	Contact report!
Elliott:	Flesh burning, like acid eating away … my face … help me …
All:	Man down!
Ash:	I've been training my whole life for this
All lads:	He's been hit!
Ash:	What's his status?
Joe:	Dead … he's dead.
All:	We have a KIA over.
Emma & Meg:	No not him, please, God, no …
Joe:	(*rocking back and forth as though traumatised and talking to himself, almost inaudible*) Do me a favour, tell me mam I fought well today.
Ash:	(*to* Brad) They're coming … just hang in there bit longer …
Emma:	(*to audience*) But he couldn't …
All:	Killed in action.
Elliott:	Losing consciousness … all goes quiet … my wife … she's expecting …
All:	We need aid, OVER!
Meg:	Will he be ok? Well, how bad is it?
All lads:	For queen and country …
All:	… Lest we forget.

Scene 4

Meg:	(*to Elliott, as though at his bedside*) It's OK … I'm here … shh now … you fell asleep.
Elliott:	I was dreaming … I was …

Meg:	Shh now ... just a bad dream ...
Elliott:	Where's the baby?
Meg:	Mum's looking after him.
Elliott:	How is he?
Meg:	He's fine, always hungry, can't feed him enough, going to be a strong lad just like his dad ... he looks just like you.
Elliott:	Like I did, you mean.
Meg:	No mistaking who he is. Wait till you see him ...
Elliott:	No ... not yet ...
Meg:	He needs his dad, Elliott.
Elliott:	Not like this he doesn't. Why would I want my own son to see me like this? I can't even bear you being here ...
Meg:	I want to be here ... it'll be alright, Elliott, there's lots they can do these days, reconstructive surgery ...
Elliott:	My face will never be the same again.
All lads:	Forever to bear the scars of a bloody war.
Meg:	Please, Elliott, you've got to stay positive.
Elliott:	Positive? I wish I'd died too, Meg, I wish it was me whose body was being flown back to our green and pleasant land in a box.
Meg:	Don't talk like that.
Elliott:	But it's true. I can't look at myself in the mirror, I don't recognise myself anymore. I can't hold my own son and look into his eyes and promise him I'll look after him forever, I can't stand my own wife looking at me. This is not the face of the man you married, Meg. Walk away ...
Meg:	What?
Elliott:	I'm giving you the chance to walk away.
Meg:	I don't want to walk away, you're my husband, the same old Elliott, and I still love you as much as the day I married you.
Elliott:	But I'm not, am I? I'm not the same ...
All lads:	Forever to bear the scars of a bloody war.
	Lads wearing half masks begin to slowly walk forward as though tired, trudging on and wounded, ghost-like.
Meg:	Same eyes that sparkled as we flirted back then ...
Elliott:	I saw the charred soldier's face, in the ruins of this war-torn place.

Meg:	Same ears that heard me whisper, 'I love you'.
Elliott:	His face just like a melted mask, the trophy of an enemy blast.
Meg:	Same lips that said, 'I do'.
Elliott:	Excuse a skull, half roast, half bone. My mind it moves to thoughts of home ...
Meg:	Same heart that still beats and flutters when we are close.
Elliott:	For how will they receive me there? The hero with a face to scare ...
Meg:	No, nothing has changed, you are still and always will be my husband, the father of my child.
Elliott:	What would he want with a father like me?
All:	Silently we pray.

Scene 5

The coffin is slowly carried forward to 'The Day Thou Gavest'. This plays throughout the following lines ...

Emma: (*to audience*) They said he was a hero. They lined the streets to pay their respects. I walked behind his coffin, which was draped in the Union Jack. He died fighting for his country, doing the job he loved. What about the woman he loved? Did he think about me when he sacrificed his life? Selfish pig ...

Brad: (*as ghost*) I loved you.

Emma: I know you did (*Cast form corridor, which she walks down. The coffin is created via body as props.*) Under the tree that Christmas, a small box, a recurring dream of mine, the moment I'd been waiting for. I walk slowly towards it, my heart pounds, I reach for it, this is it ...

Ash: (*hands* Emma *a box*) His belongings. We've returned his belongings.

Emma: No, not that box, that's the wrong box ... (*She opens it.*) My letters, photos ... like I'd been there with him ...

Brad: You have no idea how much they meant. Even during the darkest of times, you were there, always with me.

Emma: So why did you leave me then? Why didn't you think of yourself for once? Always putting others before yourself, protecting your men. Why didn't you protect me? Why didn't you think of me?

Brad: The call of duty, me or them? Always put the men beneath you before you. Their welfare, their families, everything must come before you.

Emma: What about me? (*To audience*) I know he'd have proposed that Christmas, I'm sure of it. There could never be anyone else. He was the one, mum.

Scene 6

Meg: (*tries to hand baby to* Elliott) Here, hold him.

Elliott: I can't.

Meg: You can, Elliott . . . here, I'll pass him to you.

Elliott: I can't . . . I just can't . . . not yet . . .

Meg: He's your son, he needs his dad.

Elliott: You just don't get it, do you, Meg? I don't want to be the one to give my own son nightmares!

Meg mimes placing baby down in cot.

All: Shhh, daddy will be home soon.

Meg: (*to audience*) Our firstborn, it should have been such an exciting time but all that's happened is that this little bundle of joy has added to the heartache. When Elliott returned from Afghanistan the doctors told me that the burns he had sustained to his face were irredeemable and they prepared me for the severity of his appearance, but nothing could have prepared me for the extent of his disfigurement. Remember he's watching you to see how you react, they told me. Look beyond the wounds, Meg, look for the man you married, the father of your child. (*To* Elliott) He'll love you no matter what, Elliott, you're his dad.

Cross-cut to Amy, Joe *and* Peter.

Amy: (*to* Joe) A role model, your brother looks up to you, Joe . . .

Joe: I can't look up, mam, I can't look up to anything 'cos when I open my eyes the things I see you'll never understand.

All: Constant nightmares.

Amy: I just want my son back.

Joe: I just want to forget.

All lads: Lest we forget . . .

Ash: (*sat as though begging, counting number of dead soldiers who have been brought home*) 204, 205, 2 . . . (*To passer-by*) Spare change? Ta . . . Spare change? Have a nice day. What's that look for? Head down, hurry past. Is that how we treat ex-serviceman, is it? Is that all that's down for those who fought for queen and country, is it? When you pass me by do you pity me, or loathe me? Do you frown upon my audacity to sit and beg? Do you wonder for a second who I am, what my story is?

All: Head down, hurry past . . .

Ash: Does it ever cross your mind that I may have fought for you?

Elliott: Shed the sweat of fear for you.

Joe: Dodged the hail of bullets for you.

Brad: Died for you.

Ash: No home, no job, nothing left. The bionic man, the machine, the robot.

Amy: They break you down, tear you into little pieces. When my son returned from Afghanistan he was like a different person. I just couldn't reach him. I would hear his cries in the night but couldn't do anything to help him. They break you down, tear you into little pieces.

Ash: Make a soldier of you. Make a man of you. But then what about when you return?

Elliott: To our green and pleasant land.

Ash: What do you do with us then, eh?

All: The prisoners of war.

Ash: Is this what you call hero worship, is it?

All: (*whisper*) 204, 205, 206 . . .

Ash: If only I'd have been the 207th, eh? Why didn't you take me?

All: The pride of Britain!

A: That's right, the troops have returned.

B: British soldiers back home!

C: Streets lined with people desperate to show their gratitude . . .

D: Their respect and appreciation . . .

All: Well done lads!

*As the following poem is read by the girls, the lads get into the
following positions:* **Ash** *head in hands,* **Joe** *hands over ears,* **Elliott**
hand to face, **Brad** *salute then down to floor . . .*

All girls: You smug-faced crowds with kindling eye,
Who cheer when soldier lads march by,
Sneak home and pray you'll never know,
The hell where youth and laughter go.

Meg: Why didn't you bring them home sooner?

Amy: Put an end to the war.

All lads: Only the dead will see an end to war.

Peter: And for those who return . . .

Elliott: . . . The ongoing hell, the never-ending battle.

Ash: The nightmares constant and vivid.

Joe: The wounds they can heal. But what about the mind?

All: What have I got left now?

Joe: Battle on, fight alone, but who's here to help us, Mr Prime Minister?

All: Forever bearing the scars of a bloody war . . .

Ash: There are those that return . . .

Brad: There are those who do not.

All lads: Remember us?

All: Lest we forget . . .

*'Spirit of the Glen' plays. As track plays we see: All salute, then into
position;* **Elliott** *goes to hold baby but arms turn to holding gun;*
Brad *on one knee about to propose, then head goes down as though
ducking from shell fire;* **Peter** *and* **Amy** *reach out to put hands on*
Joe's *shoulder,* **Joe** *turns and looks but then pushes their hands away;*
Ash *punches air victoriously, then hand reaches forward as though
begging for help. All girls wave then pray. All lads slowly rise from
their image, turn to front, salute and stare forward. Projection in background showing footage of soldiers who have lost their lives.*

PATHWAY 1: KS3 – AN EXPLORATORY APPROACH FOR YOUNGER LEARNERS

Workshop 1: Joe's Story – exploring the character of Joe using a variety of characterisation techniques

> **Resources needed for this workshop**
>
> Copies of the opening scene of *Lest We Forget*.

As a starter activity, read the opening scene of the play and discuss Joe's character – in particular, ask the class to focus on the acting techniques required to bring Joe 'alive' on stage. What performance skills might be needed to successfully portray Joe (voice, facial expression, body language, movement, etc.)?

In pairs, ask the learners to devise a short scene between Joe and one other character in the play which could take place before he joins the army. Ask the groups to focus on what Joe is like as a person at this time, and how to portray this character at this point in his story. As a class, create *success criteria* for effective characterisation – for instance, the use of voice in terms of *tone, pace, pitch* and *volume*; the use of *facial expression, gesture* and *movement*; how *body language* can convey emotion or relationships with other characters.

Share the work, and refer back to the 'success criteria' previously established for characterisation. Ask learners to focus on successful portrayals of Joe. Why were they successful? Which particular skills were used well?

Ask the class to consider how joining the army might alter Joe's character. Why was it considered by other characters to be *the making of him*? What does actually happen to him?

It may be helpful here to use *hot-seating* – of key characters in Joe's life – to further explore his character. Ask the learners to consider which characters they might select to be hot-seated, and what sort of questions they might like to ask. Once the exercise is completed, ask the group to consider what new information about Joe it revealed.

Using the information gathered during these introductory activities, place learners in groups of four to create a scene that illustrates a key moment of impact in Joe's life – perhaps a moment that was the 'turning point' for his character. Ask learners to consider how to portray his character in order to mark the contrast with Joe before he joined the army. Encourage groups to consider using strategies such as *spoken thought, narration* or *mini-monologue* to enhance their pieces.

An extension or alternative task could be to explain to learners that Joe kept a letter hidden under his pillow. Ask them to consider who might have written the letter, and what it may contain. This can be undertaken as a solo task, whereby learners sit in a space alone and write the letter that they later share with the class.

Extended learning

As a consolidation task, ask the group to summarise their learning today in the form of a news headline, which is spoken aloud. Ask them to complete *learner's logs*, where they can expand on their choice of headline.

Workshop 2: 'Helmand Province' – blocking, creating extension

> **Resources needed for this workshop**
>
> Copies of *Lest We Forget* play script (Scene 2).

Ask learners to study a section of *Lest We Forget* and focus on the key components of the play script. Discuss these elements as a class, paying attention to layout, punctuation, dialogue and stage directions.

Read Scene 2 from 'Touch down. Helmand Province' to '. . . should get home for the birth'.

Ask learners to consider what action is taking place as the soldiers exchange dialogue. As there is little stage direction here, they may need to consider what stage directions they might like to add – perhaps to clarify what is going on in the scene for a group of younger or less experienced actors.

Place learners in groups of four or five and ask them to annotate the scene, paying particular attention to action, vocal technique and *proxemics*. They may also like to consider how the raucous flashback scene might be presented. Is there a second flashback sequence that they could show to highlight the characters' lives before active service?

Once scripts have been annotated and the stage directions added, ask each group to swap with another, who will now interpret the stage directions on the scripts they receive. Allow time to stage the scenes. Groups can present their interpretation of this scene whilst the rest of the class evaluate the effectiveness of their performances.

If the scene were to end at '. . . might get home for the birth', could the groups consider an extension? Key questions to consider might be:

- What might happen next?
- Where could the action shift to?

- Which characters are involved?

- What dialogue and action could take place?

Ask each group to script their own extension to the scene. An alternative task is to ask groups to improvise this scene without scripting first – particularly if this is necessary to support less confident writers.

Extended learning

As a consolidation or extension task, share and evaluate the effectiveness of the pieces.

Workshop 3: The impact of war – exploring the impact of war using the strategy of *cross-cutting*

Resources needed for this workshop

Copies of *Lest We Forget* play scripts.

Paper and pens.

Begin the workshop by reading the girls' monologues (p. 101 and p. 102), and discuss how different people depicted in the play – and beyond – might be affected by war.

In groups of five, ask learners to create a group statue entitled 'Our War'. The aim is to find an economical method of capturing or representing the effect that war might have on different individuals. Half the class are then asked to present their work, whilst the other half analyse the 'statues' and try to 'read' them for what they symbolise, and what they say about the impact of war.

Explain what is meant by the drama technique of *cross-cutting*, and discuss its potential effectiveness or function within a play. Ask learners to consider how this strategy might be used; for instance, to highlight the impact of war on different people. The concept of *dramatic irony* could be considered here as a possible outcome of the exercise. For example, as a mother boasts to friends at home about how well her son is adapting to army life, we may cross-cut to a scene showing his struggles at the front.

Place learners in larger groups of six to eight, and ask them to choose two or three sets of characters who may in some way be affected by the war. The task is to find interesting methods of cross-cutting from one group of characters to the other. Examples might be:

War

- The war zone in Afghanistan cutting to families back in the UK.
- A scene of the Afghan people cutting to British troops.
- A UK politician's speech cutting to troops on the frontline.

In order to consolidate this task, groups are asked to share and evaluate the effectiveness of the pieces in terms of what they revealed about the impact of war. Encourage learners to reflect on the extent to which contrasts, comparisons and *dramatic irony* might have been created by this technique.

Extended learning

As an extension task, ask learners to reconsider the statue entitled 'Our War' which they created at the start of the workshop, and ask them to draw on paper a new, updated version of the statue. The purpose of this is to chart how their thinking might have altered because of the work explored in the workshop. Learners now have the opportunity to add a caption or title to their statue.

Work may be shared with a learning buddy or the whole class.

Workshop 4: 'Forever to bear the scars of a bloody war'

> **Resources needed for this workshop**
>
> Copies of *Lest We Forget* play script.
>
> Projection of line from play or large caption.
>
> Lighting and sound equipment, if available.
>
> Projections of images of soldiers or enlarged photographs.

As an initial *pre-set*, project the line from the play, 'Forever to bear the scars of a bloody war', and enhance the mood if possible with lights and sound. Place a plain mask in a central position as part of the pre-set together with other symbolic props; for example, a national flag, a photograph of a soldier, etc.

Ask learners to consider the line, 'Forever to bear the scars of a bloody war'.

Key questions are:

- What does this phrase mean to you?
- Why does the playwright choose to repeat this phrase at a number of points in the play?

Learners are now shown a series of images of soldiers and are asked to think of key words or phrases that they might associate with these images.

To launch the next activity, project or present *contrasting* images of injured or wounded soldiers. Ask learners what words or phrases that are now brought to mind. Use this exercise as a basis for discussion about the 'scars' that soldiers may be left with after active service.

Read the first exchange between Meg and Elliott (p. 99). Ask learners to focus on the dialogue in the scene and the way tension is created.

To extend this discussion, ask the group to consider methods of staging of the scene in order to enhance the tension between the two characters. In groups of three, learners are asked to experiment with ways of presenting the scene between Meg and Elliott. Two learners take on the roles of Meg and Elliott whilst the third acts as director or 'outside eye' who advises and directs the scene.

Once groups have explored the scene for five minutes, ask them now to experiment without dialogue, so that more attention is paid to space and physicality. Encourage learners to consider the emotional impact of the scene, and how tension might be created using this silent technique. Spotlight some groups and point out good examples of work in order to model desired outcomes.

Having established the basic staging and physical action of the scene, groups now experiment with vocal effects and different ways of delivering the dialogue, for example:

- Whispered, as though afraid of being overheard
- Angrily or confrontationally
- As though terrified
- In a cold and unfeeling manner.

Having explored staging, physicality, and now vocal effects, groups are now asked to return to the script and add in the dialogue or develop some of their own.

Once learners have experimented with a variety of ways of presenting the scene, ask them to select their most effective work and refine it before presenting to the class.

Extended learning

As an extension task, groups could add another character to the scene, thus enabling them to introduce another perspective, and alter its dynamics. This would enable the third member of the group, who has so far acted as director, to take a performance role.

Workshop 5: 'The ongoing hell, the never-ending battle . . .'

> **Resources needed for this workshop**
>
> Copies of *Lest We Forget* play script.
>
> A projection of the poem (p. 104) from the *Lest We Forget* play script.

Begin the workshop by reading or projecting the poem 'Pray you'll never know the hell, where youth and laughter go', and generate responses to the lines. Ask learners to work in groups and record their responses as a *mind map*, and then share their thoughts. What words or images spring to mind?

The discussion should now focus on the use of *imagery* and *symbolism* in the poem, and the figurative or metaphorical use of the term 'hell':

- What constitutes this 'hell'?
- What would we see or hear if we could 'get inside' a soldier's head after they had witnessed front-line action?
- Can they highlight any key lines or moments in the play which might reveal how these soldiers are affected or might feel?
- How might this 'hell' be represented on stage (for example, through the use of *montage* techniques, or using *choral speech* or *soundscape*)?

Ask learners to take up a position in the space and assume the role of a soldier on active service for the first time. Ask them to consider the moment they first arrived in a war zone. When tapped on the shoulder, they should speak the thoughts of the soldier at this point.

Now direct learners to take up contrasting positions – as the same soldier – but after he/she has returned from the front. Repeat the *thought tapping* exercise, but this time ask learners to speak the thoughts of the soldier on his or her return. Discuss how the thoughts and feelings – or indeed, personalities – of the individuals may have been altered by their experiences.

In groups of four or five, set learners the task of devising a stage representation of the soldiers' 'hell' using non-naturalistic performance techniques. A 'menu' of non-naturalistic strategies can be devised with the class before they start the task. Techniques could include:

- The use of *still image* or *tableaux vivants*
- Sudden changes of *pace* and *rhythm*
- The use of *soundscape* or sound effects

- *Choral speech* techniques: whispering, echo or chanting
- *Slow motion*
- Exaggerated *movement, mime and gesture*
- *Cross-cutting* or *simultaneous staging*
- The use of *space and levels* to create tension or emphasise status.

After sufficient working time, share the pieces and evaluate them in terms of their theatrical effect.

Extended learning

As an extension task, ask learners to write their own poem exploring the *ongoing hell, the never-ending battle of the inner mind.*

Workshop 6: 'Read it in the papers, saw it on the news'

> **Resources needed for this workshop**
>
> Newspaper for *pre-set.*

Start the workshop with a *pre-set* of a newspaper, placed centrally in the space. Instruct learners to move around the space. When a number is called they must quickly get into groups of that number and create *still images* to represent the following headlines:

- 'Troops Return Home'
- 'Streets Lined with People Paying Their Respects'
- 'Heroes Send Off as Troops Leave for Helmand Province'
- 'Frontline Casualties'.

Each group now chooses one of the headlines to 'bring to life' for 30 seconds of action. Share the work, and encourage reflection on media representations of war.

For their next task, ask groups to create a *news documentary* based on their knowledge and understanding of the play, and the events that took place in Afghanistan. Encourage groups to explore the use of:

- Different vantage points and perspectives
- *Direct address* to camera/audience

War

- *Hot-seating/Interview* of one or more characters
- *Flashbacks* caught on camera.

Share and evaluate the work.

Extended learning

As an extension task, the pieces could be developed further and filmed using digital video cameras, to be presented as part of a media/ICT project entitled 'Images of War'.

PATHWAY 2: KS4 – A PERFORMANCE-SKILLS APPROACH FOR OLDER LEARNERS

Workshop 1: Blocking a key scene

This workshop allows learners to experiment with the staging of a scene and create an extension of it from a playwright's, director's and actor's point of view.

Resources needed for this workshop

Copies of Scene 4 of the play *Lest We Forget*.

Pens and paper.

Building blocks

Read Scene 4 of the play, from 'We were under attack' to the end, and ask learners to consider ways of blocking the scene. (You may need to clarify the meaning of 'blocking' first.) Allow time to experiment with ways of blocking the scene.

Now give learners different ways of presenting this section of script. Allow a short amount of time for them to experiment with each new perspective:

- Present at a very fast pace
- Present as though very angry
- Present as though sharing a huge secret
- Present in the style of a news documentary
- Present in silence using movement, mime and gesture only.

Discuss the groups' responses to the task – how experimenting in this way might have altered their perspective on the scene, or enabled them to develop their performance skills.

Using knowledge and understanding gained from the previous task, learners are now asked to work in groups and annotate the section of script they have just worked on. They should be encouraged to add in stage directions that notate the actors' use of movement, gesture and voice as well as how space might be utilised.

The challenge

Learners must now script an extension to the scene and add in detailed stage directions which make it very clear how they imagine their scene to be performed. Encourage learners to adopt the perspective of playwright or director during this task.

Top tips/Ask the expert

Groups now swop their work with another group. The aim here is for learners to interpret the writing and stage direction of others. Allocate sufficient time for groups to work on staging their new scripts.

Re-focus and refine

Groups are now given the opportunity to give and receive feedback on the scripts they have developed. This is an ideal opportunity for learners to hear – and perhaps see – how effectively their scripts were interpreted by others.

Ideas for improvement should be exchanged between groups. After this feedback session groups return to their own scripts and make the necessary adjustments in accordance with the feedback received.

Workshop 2: Effective use of symbolism

This workshop provides learners with an opportunity to use higher-order thinking skills as they explore the use of symbolism in the play.

Resources needed for this workshop

A large Union flag.

A selection of 'symbolic' stage props.

Building blocks

Place a large Union flag (UK national flag) centre stage, and ask learners to consider what it symbolises or represents for them. Introduce the key term *symbolism*, and if necessary provide simple examples of how visual symbols might be used in theatre; for example, how a character wearing black might be 'read' as evil, or a chain might represent imprisonment or oppression (negative) or coming together (positive), or perhaps how symbolic gestures (a clenched fist or pointed finger) might be used to symbolise aggression, power or solidarity.

Ask learners to form groups of five or six and create both a 'positive' and 'negative' still image that in both cases uses the Union flag symbolically.

Images should be shared and evaluated. If necessary to clarify meaning, ask groups to bring each image to life briefly using their own choice of drama strategy.

The challenge

In the same groups, ask learners to select a visual symbol of their own which could be incorporated into a section from the play – this could be either an object (stage prop) or gesture.

Top tips/Ask the expert

Each group is now asked to present their section of the play incorporating their choice of symbol.

For each scene presented, ask the audience members to reflect and comment on:

- The groups' choice of symbol
- Its meaning or function within the scene
- Its effect: In what ways did it enhance the scene? How might its use be made more effective?

Re-focus and refine

With this feedback in mind, learners should now be given an opportunity to reflect upon their use of symbolism and, if necessary, develop their work further. Ask learners to reflect upon their use of symbolism and its effectiveness in performance. Can they find other examples of the use of symbols in drama – perhaps in film or TV dramas with which they are familiar?

Workshop 3: Performance support – stage design

> **Resources needed for this workshop**
>
> Diagram of stage areas.
>
> Materials for creating simple stage designs, e.g. squared paper and pencils, model-making materials, simple computer software.

Building blocks

As an introductory exercise, show the group a diagram of stage areas (Resource sheet 1).

Ask learners to take up a position in the space and, on the teacher's instruction, move to the designated area of the stage. Further develop this to set simple images to be created in particular areas of the stage, for example: *upstage right: Ash begging on the street; downstage centre: in the war zone.*

Having familiarised the group with stage areas, in groups of four or five, ask the learners to list the locations identified in the script.

Ask the groups to consider where the various locations identified could be positioned on stage and to present this as a plan of the space, which can be annotated and explained to the rest of the group.

The challenge

The main task is to design a multi-functional set for the play, which can be easily transported for an 'end-on' touring production of the play.

They will need to consider:

- The use of stage blocks or rostra to create levels and stage settings
- Use of backdrops, flats or projections to provide visual images
- Entrances and exits
- The use of multi-functional props.

Designs could be presented simply on paper as plans, or as three-dimensional models, or using computer software. Groups should prepare a short presentation of their ideas, which will be pitched to the whole group.

Resource sheet 1

	AUDIENCE	
DOWNSTAGE LEFT	DOWNSTAGE CENTRE	DOWNSTAGE RIGHT
STAGE LEFT	CENTRE STAGE	STAGE RIGHT
UPSTAGE LEFT	UPSTAGE CENTRE	UPSTAGE RIGHT

Re-focus and refine

Explain to the groups that the director of the play has now decided to present the play 'in the round'. Ask them to return to their groups and adapt their designs to accommodate this. Again, these ideas may be shared. As an extension task, groups are now asked to select one scene from the play and to experiment with staging it 'in the round'.

Workshop 4: 'Everyone has a story to tell'

This workshop enables learners to take more ownership of the play as they develop their own characters and stories and explore ways of expanding and developing the piece.

Resources needed for this workshop

Four character name labels.

Building blocks

Before the lesson, prepare the space by dividing it into four areas marked with a character name – Brad, Elliot, Joe, Ash.

On entry, ask learners to move to one of the four areas, and with their group share as much information as they have gained so far about this particular character. Extend this by pooling information with the whole group in order to summarise the groups' understanding.

Bring the learners back together and ask them to consider 'significant others' – characters who do not appear in the play, but could be connected in some way to characters that do. For example, a member of Ash's family who is not referred to in the play itself, or a doctor who may have treated Joe or Elliot on their return to the UK.

Ask each learner to select a character who in some way is linked to one of the soldiers in the play. Ask them to imagine that a film crew are making a documentary about these main characters and in order to do so are interviewing 'significant others' in their lives. Each character will be asked to give a statement – *as though direct to camera* – about their relationship or involvement with the character from the play. (Some learners may feel more comfortable preparing this on paper in advance.)

Once learners have made their preparations they are grouped as follows: anyone whose significant other is connected to Brad moves back to the area of the space designated for that character at the start of the lesson. In turn, ask learners to move to the space for Elliot, Ash or Joe.

War

Once groups have been formed around each character, each learner will in turn present their statement 'to camera'. It may be useful to place a chair centrally in each area for this purpose.

Encourage the groups to discuss the presentations once the cycle is complete. Key questions might be:

- Did any character stand out or make a particular impact?
- Did any of the statements suggest an interesting *back story* relating to the character?
- Which character might be best to develop further?

The challenge

Based on the insights gained from the above exercise, ask students, working in small groups, to develop the 'back story' relating to the characters they have begun to create. Is there a particular incident or scene that could be devised based around this character? In order to facilitate this, students take it in turns to direct the other group members in a short, improvised scene concerning 'their' character.

Top tips/Ask the expert

There is opportunity here for groups to share their work-in-progress in order to receive feedback on ways in which they might further enhance and develop their pieces. One effective method of doing this is for the class to watch each piece in turn and decide – as a whole class – which character or scenario they would most like to 'add' into the play. This strategy provides an opportunity for all groups to perform, but also encourages learners to take on the perspectives of directors or playwrights who must make decisions regarding the development of the play.

Re-focus and refine

During this phase, learners focus upon how they might incorporate their new character or scenario into the rest of the play. There are opportunities here to consider the 'new' scene in relation to other scenes in the play, and use other class members as directors.

In this role they are able to:

- Give advice about the new scene and make any necessary amendments.
- Consider the various options for incorporating the new section to the existing script – whereabouts in the play might it be most effectively placed?
- Test out the choices made in performance – perhaps by 'workshopping' alternatives – to ensure that the new version of the play 'works' in practice.

Workshop 5: The homecoming

This workshop provides an opportunity for learners to use non-verbal communi-
cation/physical theatre as a method of storytelling.

Resources needed for this workshop

Copies – or projection – of Amy's monologue from the final scene of *Lest We Forget*.

Paper and pens.

Building blocks

Read Amy's monologue in the final scene:

> They break you down, tear you into little pieces. When my son returned from
> Afghanistan he was like a different person. I just couldn't reach him. I would hear his
> cries in the night but couldn't do anything to help him. They break you down, tear you
> into little pieces.

Ask learners to sit alone and draw on paper the image that best reflects Joe's
inner thoughts on return from Afghanistan. The rule here is that Joe must be
represented somewhere on the paper. However, the images do not have to be
literal or naturalistic – more abstract ideas can be used, for instance metaphors
(... *he's at a crossroads* ...) or symbols (e.g. a *storm cloud* or *cliff edge*) can be
introduced, or colour can be used symbolically. To develop this further (and for
those who are not confident at drawing!) words or annotations can be added to
the images.

Learners share their drawings with one or two others. They should be encouraged to explain and justify their work. This can shared with the whole class if
time allows.

Discuss the impact that active service might have had on Joe – and, by inference,
many other soldiers. Key questions are:

- How has life altered for them?

- How might their personality or beliefs have changed?

- What experiences might have affected them or altered their perspective on
  life?

This exercise can clearly build on work explored in the previous workshop.

At this point the class are asked to consider the value of non-verbal communi-
cation and what techniques they might need to draw upon; for example,

movement, mime and gesture, figurative mime (*body as props*), the symbolic use of space and levels or variations in pace. (A clip of the Hungarian physical theatre group *Attraction* – or the work of similar companies – could be shown at this point as a demonstration of what is possible.)

The challenge

In groups of four or five, learners are asked to create a non-verbal/physical theatre piece that is entitled *The Homecoming*. The piece should chart the change in the soldier from leaving for active service to their homecoming. It should reflect how the soldier's experiences of war have had an impact on their lives and the contrast in that soldier from before to after they return.

Top tips/Ask the expert

Groups share their work with one other group in order to gain feedback on the clarity of meaning, the effectiveness of techniques used and how they might enhance the piece.

Re-focus and refine

Using the feedback given, each group now has the opportunity to adapt or develop their work. They might also now wish to consider the impact of sound and/or music, multi-media enhancements such as projections and effective use of the performance space. The work could be developed further through the simple use of shadow theatre or puppetry. These techniques can be particularly effective in developing sections of the work that are technically difficult – for instance, problems in portraying journeys, changes in perspective or scale, or abstract effects can all be resolved through these approaches.

   Learners should perform their pieces and evaluate the effectiveness of their work.

Workshop 6: A 'raising awareness' event

Resources needed for this workshop

Pens and paper for planning.

This central idea could be developed into a series of workshops as it provides learners with the opportunity to plan, rehearse, produce and carry out an event based around the play.

Building blocks

Learners are asked to consider the ways that as a society we become aware of the plight of soldiers and the impact that war has upon them and their families.

The challenge

Learners are informed that they have been commissioned to produce an evening event that raises awareness of the impact that war can have upon soldiers. In groups they must plan out a programme that could be used to highlight some of the key issues raised in the play. They must consider the title of the event, what exactly it must include and how they are going to advertise or promote it. They must create their own performance piece which can be shown on the night and perhaps consider other aspects of performance which could be incorporated into the event.

Top tips/Ask the expert

There is opportunity here for learners to research other theatre companies or local charities in order to liaise with outside agencies. This would also allow an opportunity for a more vocational focus.

The planning and rehearsal process for this event is really at your discretion. How the event is evaluated/quality assured is also an issue for consideration.

Re-focus and refine

There may be various moments throughout the rehearsal process when learners are asked to reflect upon the progress of the event and areas for development. Pitching their ideas to yourself or perhaps an outside agency could be another avenue to explore. Groups may use the idea of 'The Boardroom' whereby they meet at regular intervals to reflect, amend, discuss and re-focus their ideas and roles within the project.

Riot

Introduction and context

The horrifying events which unfolded on the streets of Britain between 6 and 10 August 2011 – mass rioting and looting in the streets of many major towns and cities, and the aftermath of burned buildings and wrecked businesses – are widely regarded as the worst UK example of civil unrest in living memory. Watched by millions on TV as they unfolded, the riots and their 'causes' have been much debated, and the legislative response to the mostly young people involved was quick and decisive, with many being sent to prison for long periods. Some of the statistics are interesting for what they might tell us about those who took part in the riots: of the 1,984 people brought before the courts, 90 per cent of those arrested were male and 13 per cent were regarded as 'gang members, 42 per cent were white, 53 per cent black or Asian (with 5 per cent recorded as 'other'), and about half were under the age of 21. Two-thirds of the young people brought to court were regarded as having some kind of special educational need, and about the same proportion already had a previous criminal conviction or caution. More than a third of the young people had been excluded from school in the previous year, and 42 per cent claimed free school meals – a reliable indicator of poverty.

In this unit learners will have an opportunity to explore the events of August 2011 through the eyes of nine different characters who were all in some way involved. Workshops allow learners to work directly with the structure and performance of monologues on which the play is based. They also enable them to engage with the controversies surrounding what took place on those evenings through the thoughts and feelings of those involved.

One Summer Evening – The play

> **A note from the playwrights**
>
> Although we believe that this piece makes a satisfying short play as it stands, this sequence of monologues is intended to provide the 'bones' of a more developed text for performance, so that learners might use it as a starting point for their own explorations.
>
> The characters in the play present their own perspectives on the events of August 2011 and many of the words that they speak are based upon actual testimony – or commentary – provided as the events unfolded and in their aftermath.
>
> JR and KW

One Summer Evening

Kirsty Walters and John Rainer

Cast

Youth
Police officer
Local business owner A
Local business owner B
Mother
Politician
Police officer's wife
Bystander
Sociologist

1. Youth – 1st monologue

When I was a kid, in the winter, ants would come into the house. My mam would try and find the nest, and pour a kettle of boiling water over it – but it never did any good.

I used to put an apple core down on the tiles round the gas fire, and within minutes, there'd be hundreds of 'em, like a seething black crust.

I used to take one or two. And put 'em on the gas ring – in the middle of the biggest burner. As they walked to the edge I'd ignite the gas, and see them frizzle. An' I'd do it again, and again ...

I didn't plan to rob anything.

We were just having a look – had a text on my Blackberry saying it was all kicking off – and went down to see. I never even took a bag with me ...

It started with smashing the security grill. Within minutes there's loads of people ducking inside and helping themselves.

And one of them asked me what size trainers I wore ...

There were women with shopping trolleys, guys parking up vans, unloading the whole shop ... and then moving on to the next one.

And you know what? It felt good.

When the police arrived, you could tell they was scared. And it was, 'Let's cause frickin' chaos, let's cause a riot'.

And then people started having a go – throwing stuff an' taunting 'em an' that. And then the car went up in flames and people scattered ... and then moved on to the next shop, and the next.

And I thought, 'If we want to do this, we can. And you won't do nothing. You can't do nothing to stop us'.

And we began to realise. If we spread this, could the police control it?

It was like turning the gas on and lighting it. And it felt good.

Really, really good.

2. Police officer – 1st monologue

It was the scariest thing that's ever happened to me.

Things moved so quickly we couldn't follow what was happening. It was obvious that they were communicating with each other – they'd all be in one place and we would get a message, but by the time we got there they were away – they'd break up into smaller groups and just disappear. So officers got frustrated. We weren't able to respond. The training manual does not tell you what to do in this kind of situation. And then we got cornered between two office blocks – there was about thirty . . . forty of them.

I received a blow to the head from a flying brick, and it split my NATO-issue public order helmet. I could feel the blood trickling down my neck – but what can you do? There was no one going to come to our assistance, and I remember thinking I had to keep going. If I'd have gone down, that would have been it.

The bricks were coming thick and fast, and they were organised: they'd stolen some shopping trolleys from the Tesco's across the street, and were using them to replenish their stocks of things to throw . . . bringing trolley loads of bricks and debris from a building site.

And then an elderly woman – just crossing the street – got hit in the face, and went down. We grouped around her, to try and protect her – but they kept on throwing stuff – bloody great big chunks of masonry. They didn't care about this poor woman. They had no sense of decency. We charged with our shields drawn, so that the ambulance could get to her. I've never seen anybody look as terrified as that ambulance driver.

They knew we were scared of them. And yes, they would have killed us.

There was nothing left to steal or smash, and so they turned on us . . .

3. Local business owners

A: Strike the match, start the fire, watch it burn. The walls of the palace come crumbling down into a pile of ashes that resemble nothing of the past. Just memories of what once was.

B: I read in the paper that the cost to business and the taxpayer came to 500 million pounds. I spent 30 years building this business. My father started it, and handed it to me and my brother.

A: My Gran and I always had a special relationship. She bragged to everyone she knew about me, and was proud as punch when I went off to uni to study fashion design. When she died she left money for me to achieve my dreams. It was enough to open a small business. A shop where my designs could be displayed, and sold. It was only a small business, but it was mine.

B: We are not get-rich-quick merchants, rip-off bankers, fat cats. We don't drive flash cars, own big houses. We flog furniture. At a small profit. We do a good job – a good service. We give a discount to OAPs. 'Responsible capitalism', they call it. I can understand people being angry. Kids, with no hope and no job. But they were animals, that night. They smashed their way in and stole what they could carry. They were in frenzy. What would a 15-year-old lad want with a reclining armchair? Then they set a fire, and within minutes it was all gone.

A: As news of the riots spread across town, I got that uneasy feeling that you sometimes get in the pit of your tummy when you know something's not quite right but you're not sure what it is. I got in the car and drove down there. Police had cordoned off part of the street. I stood and watched my little business in flames.

B: What's happened to the world? Nothing on telly but talent shows and celebrity rubbish. Everything's corrupt – the newspapers, the politicians, the bankers, even the police . . . Everybody's got their snout in the trough, in it for what they can make. No values. What kind of an example does it set?

A and B: Course, we can claim on the insurance. Get some of the money back.

A: The next day people pulled together – put on a united front and refused to be beaten. They cleaned the streets, swept away the debris, removed the shattered glass. I sat and could not move. Around me people busily pulled together but still I could not move. On the news they interviewed some of the rioters and they voiced their disregard for a society which apparently 'does nothing to support the likes of us'.

B: But some of them that did it live round here, walk past the shop every day. I saw their pictures. Recognised some faces, know their families. The shop . . . it was a local landmark – Robson's Corner. Young girls used to meet their boyfriends there before a night out. Handy for the Odeon across the road, you see. Those kids' parents might've sheltered from the rain under the awning. Not anymore. They can bloody well get wet . . .

A: They had apparently wanted to make people listen. I would have listened. Did they need to have done it like that?

B: I'm too old to start again. That's it.

4. Mother – 1st monologue

As a family, we did a lot together. It didn't matter that the kids were growing up, they still wanted to be involved as much as possible in family stuff. Next on the list was the camping holiday at the end of August. Emma and John had come round to discuss arrangements over a glass of wine. 'Let's write a list of what we need to take', said Emma, ever organised. The wine flowed as plans for the holiday were made. In the background the telly was on. It was the news and it was showing footage of the riots taking place in Manchester. My eyes drifted over to the telly as we talked. Such awful scenes of anarchy and chaos. What was happening to society? 'Frightening, isn't it?', remarked Emma, noticing that my attention was drawn to the screen. 'What a world we're living in,' I commented, 'these are just kids'. The conversation switched back to who would share tents. The two older boys – my son, 17, and theirs, 16 – would be better in together, the smell of two teenage lads better kept apart from the rest of us! It was then that something else caught my eye on the screen. I started to drift again into a world of violence, aggression, sheer terror, as the streets of Manchester were taken over by thugs. On the screen was a number for people to ring should they recognise the faces of any of the young people shown in the news coverage. The police urgently wanted people to come forward, to help them with their enquiries, to identify the thugs responsible for the carnage on screen. The voices of those in my lounge seemed to drift further and further away as I looked at the screen. A feeling of sweat, nausea, legs turning to jelly. Amidst all of the other faces on that screen was that of my son, Daniel. It couldn't be him, it couldn't possibly be! I looked away, then back at the screen again. No one else must see. I see, and I know those eyes. It is without doubt the child I gave birth to, the baby I held in my arms, the son I had come to regard as a companion, the apple of my eye. The message on the bottom of the screen: 'Where are your children tonight?' I jump up, fumble for the remote, switch channels quickly. 'You OK?' asks Emma, noticing my sudden change in demeanour. 'Yeah, fine, just feel a bit off'. Within no time at all, I am ushering my guests out of my house. 'Probably just an upset tummy', I lie. I close the door and my husband is concerned: 'Can I get you anything, love?' 'No thanks,' I reply, 'I probably just need an early night'. I climb the stairs, stand frozen in my bedroom. And then I try his mobile. It is switched off.

5. Politician

We have looked under a stone and revealed something about our society that we would rather not see. A seething mass of foul creatures – insects – engaged in cynical acts of materialism, hate and lawlessness.

There will be those who say that these riots are an act of revolt – presumably against the justified budget cuts enacted by the present government. However, for those who say that the riots are about a disenfranchised youth finding their voice, I say this: what we have seen in the riots in London, Manchester and other places this week is nothing more than shopping with violence. All it reveals is that young people in Britain today have a misguided sense of entitlement – they want it all without effort. They no longer have a moral compass; they have lost their way. They prove that our society is broken. It will take serious and determined efforts to fix it.

6. Police officer – 2nd monologue

The sounds are deafening, the scenes are of chaos and destruction. There is pure venom in their eyes, their body language says fight, aggression, no fear. This is not something I have experienced before. Never have I seen our city look and feel so very threatening … threatened. Many of these rioters are young people … teen-agers who behind the masks are nothing more than spotty adolescents who will return home to their homes tonight, get into bed and have no concept of the damage they have caused. In this situation a human being has a fight or flight reaction. As a police officer there is only one option, and that is to fight.

7. Police officer's wife

When you marry a police officer, you marry into the job. You accept that there are times when you say goodbye and you have no clue about where they are going to or who they are dealing with. That night was one of those times. It was my youngest daughter's fifth birthday and we were having a little gathering at our house. He was on call, which meant that there was no booze for him that night. We knew that he could be called out at any time and we were used to that. The call, in fact, came in the middle of the night. They had needed to draft in more officers as things in the city centre were getting so out of control. I was half asleep as he quickly got dressed and planted a kiss on my forehead. Don't think I even said goodbye.

8. Youth – 2nd monologue

'Come on then!'

'What you waiting for?' I'm screaming at them, the pigs. They hate us, blame us for everything. 'Come on, you bastards!' We're just taking back what the government's taken from us. Noise, loads of it. I'm buzzin'. Us and them. Hood up, balaclava on. I can see them, but they can't see me.

'Come on then!'

9. Bystander

What I want to know is why these kids are not at home with their mams and dads. They need a bloody good hiding. In my day, one step out of line and I'd have been grounded for a month. Nowadays . . . anything goes. And the language! Just listen to 'em! Some of them were only 12, 13-year-olds. Do you think anybody knows where they are, what they're up to?

I'm afraid what this boils down to is PPP: Piss-poor parenting . . .

10. Mother – 2nd monologue

I lie awake even though I pretend to be asleep when my husband comes to bed. He must not know about this. He will go mad, so I must deal with it alone until I have decided on the right course of action. When he is finally asleep, I creep downstairs. I sit in the darkness of my lounge and I wait. At 2 a.m. the door quietly clicks open. He is trying not to disturb us. He kicks off his shoes and leaves them in the hall, something I have always told him to do. Doing as he's told has never really been a problem before. You may be thinking that this is what all protective mothers might say when faced with a problem that is about to rock their world. A mother's instinct – to protect, defend, justify. I have always had a good relationship with Dan. I'm not going to lie, we have had our moments. Teenage lads rarely escape the teenage years unscathed, do they? On the whole, though, he hadn't given us any real problems. Popular, intelligent – just a good lad really. He goes into the kitchen to get himself a drink. He does not switch the light on. I stand at the kitchen door. He turns, I startle him. 'Shit, Mum, what you doing up?' 'Waiting for you', I reply, and I look deep into those familiar eyes. 'You OK?', he asks. 'Where've you been?' – my voice steady, controlled, calm. 'Just out with Nick and that', he replies, a little edgy. 'I phoned you', I say. 'More than once – but your phone was off'. He looks a little uncomfortable and does that face that he does when he is about to tell his mother a lie. 'Yeah, I didn't realise it was off. Did you need me?' I stare at him. 'Mum . . . you OK?' He is starting to get a little concerned. 'Where have you been?' I repeat. 'I've just said. I'm going to bed', he says, rattled, unsettled, defensive. He passes me as I remain stood at the door. Our eyes lock for a second. 'Come on, son,' I plead inwardly, 'please don't let me down, please make this OK'. Inside, I am begging him to give me some explanation, some reassurance, to tell me that there has been some mistake. The silence remains. He walks away and makes for the stairs. 'I saw your face on the news. I know where you were tonight', I say. My voice is quiet, almost a whisper. I cannot let my husband know what is going on. He won't deal with it right. I have to get this sorted out in my own head first. Dan looks at me, and at first his face shows an expression of confusion, he is going to try and deny it. 'I saw you Dan, involved with the riots. You were there'. He is also frozen, rooted to the spot. The air is cold, freezing cold, bone-chillingly tense. 'The police are asking for people to come forward, to name the faces shown on screen', I whisper. There is no emotion on my voice, just monotone, cold. He looks at me and the expression has now changed. There is now the face that I recognise, eyes of panic, sheer 'please mum, help me' panic. 'Mum, I can explain . . . Mum, please . . . what you going to do?' I take a step towards him. 'Go to bed, son'. 'Have you told dad?' he asks. 'I said, go to bed. We'll talk about it in the morning when I've had more time to think'. 'Have you told dad?' he repeats. I shake my head. The tears sting. 'Go to bed'. And he does.

11. Sociologist

What happened was the worst urban disorder in this country in living memory. It is crucially important to give the riots some context and to try to understand why they happened. Britain is now more unequal than any other western country apart from the United States, and the gap between rich and poor widens every year. The UK is deeply economically divided and stark and entrenched poverty exists in many areas, with devastating consequences for those who experience it. The current government's policies are making things worse by slashing the essential services on which the poorest members of society rely.

Rioting and stealing consumer goods is perhaps not a politically mature form of protest, but it may have been the only way these young people felt they could communicate the disrespect, hurt and anger that they clearly feel. Rather than dismiss these people as scum, maybe we need to try and understand. There are lots of questions left unanswered.

If what the riots show is these young people's fundamental disrespect for authority, we need to start asking: what are they angry about and who, precisely, don't they respect? And, most importantly, what can be done to help them feel part of society, with a vested interest in making it work instead of destroying it?

12. Mother – 3rd monologue

The next morning he waits until his dad has left for work before venturing down-stairs. I have to get my youngest to school, so I try to act as normal as possible as I don't want the other one picking up on any of this. I flap as I try to find my car keys, 'Where the bloody hell are they?' I mutter, and it is then I hear his voice, 'They're here'. I turn and we clap eyes on each other for the first time that morning. 'Thanks', I reply. We hold a stare for a few seconds before I look to my other son and say, 'Come on or we'll be late'. As I make for the front door I hear him mutter, 'What are you going to do?' Slowly I turn back and reply, 'I haven't decided yet'. His face, so tired, pale and pathetic. My motherly instinct is to protect, to tell the child that everything will be all right, to make things better. I cannot do that at this precise moment because the child I am staring back at is almost unrecognisable to me. I walk out of the door, get into the car and take a deep breath. After the school drop off I will sort my head out. I will rationalise, reason and regain control. I will decide what exactly I am going to do. I pull out of the drive and glance back across at the lounge window. He is staring back at me.

13. Police officer – 3rd monologue

That summer evening I experienced a side to the job that I had never experienced before. It was a feeling of powerlessness and a loss of control. It was a fear that this uniform no longer stood for anything other than a disguise that protected the man underneath it from being recognised. Flight or fight . . .

14. Mother – 4th monologue

My job: to protect. Yet that evening, those feelings became confused with disappointment, dismay, guilt. I had somehow failed in my role as a parent. Could I now fail a society that I had, for a long time, feared was being ruined by those who had been brought up unaware of the difference between right and wrong?

15. Final scene

Business owner B: Thirty years building up a business . . .

Business owner A: Which was destroyed in less than thirty minutes.

Business owners A and B: That evening . . .

Politician: They lost their way . . .

Police officer: They wanted to be listened to . . .

Bystander: The language they used!

All: That evening . . .

Youth: We wanted our voices to be heard!

Sociologist: There are important questions left unanswered . . .

Police officer's wife: And the biggest question in my mind is . . .

All: Who's to say it won't happen again?

PATHWAY 1: KS3 – AN EXPLORATORY APPROACH FOR YOUNGER LEARNERS

Workshop 1: Flag as *symbol*

Resources needed for this workshop

A large national flag.

Internet-linked projector to present YouTube clip (http://www.youtube.com/watch?v=4YYcAmSJu8A).

Place a large Union flag in the centre of the space as a *pre-set* and pose the question: 'If the flag could speak, what would it say?'

Discuss with the class their understanding of the meaning of the word *symbolism* and its use in drama.

Place learners in groups of four or five, and ask each group to create a still image that incorporates the flag in some way. After a few minutes of work time ask groups to share their work and reflect on the use of the flag as a symbol in each image.

Now ask each group to further develop their work by bringing the image to life for 30 seconds of action. This provides a good opportunity for learners to show their work and to give and receive feedback. Within the discussion/evaluation it may be helpful to draw out how national symbols such as flags are often perceived to be positive symbols of patriotism and pride, but that they can also evoke more negative connotations: did any groups use the flag to draw out a positive representation of 'the nation'? Were there images of *patriotism* or *nationalism* presented?

Ask learners to return to the pre-set and sit around it. Now alter the image by ruffling up the flag and placing a prop such as a baseball bat or armed police helmet or shield on top of it. Ask learners for their responses and to consider how their perspective may have altered.

Show the montage of the UK riots from YouTube and discuss the events of summer 2011.

Key questions to discuss with the class may be:

- What happened?
- What triggered the events?
- How did it make you feel at the time?
- Why did people choose to get involved?

- What happened as a result of it?

- How do the events of summer 2011 make you feel about living in the UK (or for those outside the UK, how do the events represent the UK and its people?)

Ask learners to return to their groups. Building on their developing understanding of the theme, they must now create a second still image which incorporates the flag in a way that is deliberately *ambiguous* or *ironic* – perhaps in a way that subverts the idea of the flag as a symbol of national pride. If necessary to clarify meaning, again this image can be developed into 30 seconds of action.

As an extension task, ask groups to find a way of capturing the essence of the summer riots through soundscape, stylised movement and dialogue.

After sharing the work, ask learners to return to the initial exercise: 'If the flag could speak now, what would it say?', and see if their response differs now.

Extended learning

To consolidate learning, ask learners to summarise their learning in the workshop in a maximum of twenty words, or, alternatively, ask other learners to choose a random number between one and ten: this number is then the maximum number of words allowed.

Workshop 2: Creating dramatic tension and exploring *Dan's* inner thoughts

Resources needed for this workshop

Mother's 1st and 2nd monologues from the play *One Summer Evening*.

Pens and paper.

Read the play with the group in order to gain an overview of the characters involved.

Ask the group to focus on the mother's 1st and 2nd monologues and discuss character purpose, motivation and attitude.

What does the text reveal about the mother, and her relationship with her son?

What is directly stated, and what might be *inferred*?

Ask learners to focus on the character of the mother and to use 'red hat thinking' in order to explore her thoughts and feelings at this stage.

Having now developed a deeper understanding of the mother's character, ask the group to consider what conversation might have taken place between the mother and Dan – her son – when he walks in that night. In doing this, ask the learners to expand on the information given in the mother's monologue – to read 'between the lines'. Target individuals to share their ideas at this stage.

Discuss the meaning of *dramatic tension* and how this might be created in the scene between the two. Ask them to list their own *success criteria* and then share with the rest of the class. Factors to consider might include:

- The actor's use of silence and the pause; eye contact, gesture, voice and intonation; pace
- The relationship between the actor and audience; proximity; configuration; staging; acting style
- The *given circumstances*: is there anything in the setting of the scene – when and where it takes place, for instance – which might create more tension?
- The use of music or sound and lighting, if available.

Put learners in pairs and ask them to improvise the scene between the mother and Dan at this point. They may need to be reminded that the scene takes place late at night with the dad and sibling asleep upstairs; does this in itself create tension?

Ask each group to share their work with another pair who can provide feedback on how to develop and/or improve the scene. Emphasise the key question: 'Did the group create dramatic tension in the scene, and if so, how? What effect did it have on the audience?'

Once the scenes have been explored and perhaps developed, ask the group to focus on *Dan's* character and how he might feel as he walks away from his mother and goes up to bed. With a volunteer to depict Dan, ask the group to provide his *spoken thoughts.*

Suggest to the group that that Dan's own monologue – which revealed his perspective on the events – has been accidentally omitted from the script, and ask them to consider what the monologue would have contained. Ask learners to work alone to script their monologues.

This is an individual task, but mid-way through the process of composing Dan's monologue ask learners to share their work in progress with a learning buddy and to give, and receive, feedback.

Key questions could be:

- What acting techniques might be most effective in capturing Dan's thoughts and feelings through this monologue?

- What advice would you give to the actor delivering the lines?
- How would they stage the scene for maximum effect?

Some learners may wish to present their work or perhaps swop with a partner and experiment with the work of someone else.

Extended learning

Complete *learner's logs*.

Workshop 3: Perspectives on the night

> **Resources needed for this workshop**
>
> Paper and pens for captions.
>
> Music to create mood and tension.
>
> Copies of Monologues 6 and 8 from the play *One Summer Evening*.

Read Monologues 6 and 8 with the class.

These monologues capture the characters 'in the moment' of the action. Imagine that a press reporter was present and captured four photographs showing what took place. In groups of four or five, ask learners to recreate these photographs via four still images. Each must depict the two key characters and capture the emotion of the events.

In order to share the work thus far, ask each group to present their images as an uninterrupted sequence of four. Sound or music could be added to create atmosphere.

To further develop their work, each group must now devise the 'headline' linked to each of their 'photographs'. These are presented as captions using paper and pens provided.

Ask the groups to represent their original sequence – but this time with the captions spoken.

Key questions to consider:

- Did the addition of the headline alter the meaning of the sequences in any way?
- Does this suggest anything about the way in which the media can manipulate 'documentary' images, or information?

Riot

As a final task, explain that CCTV footage of the events captured another image – at a 90-degree angle to the four images already devised. This revealed a completely different perspective.

Ask the students to consider what this fifth image revealed and how it contrasted to the others.

Their task is to present this new perspective via an extra still image.

Ask the groups to select one of the four original images to present as a contrast with the new, fifth image. Share the work, and leave time for reflection and feedback.

Extended learning

Complete *learner's logs*.

Workshop 4: Exploring Mother's dilemma

Resources needed for this workshop

Copies of Mother's 3rd monologue from the play *One Summer Evening*.

Read Mother's 3rd monologue and discuss her dilemma.

As a group, *hot-seat* the mother using different volunteers to portray her in order to gain different possible perspectives.

Ask the group to reflect on this exercise and note any insights gained into Mother's character or motivation.

At this point, use the strategy of whole-class *conscience alley* to explore her dilemma. Ask the group to imagine that Mother is on her way to the police station. As she walks down the 'alley' the class speak her thoughts – her inner conscience – either 'for' or 'against' reporting her son to the authorities.

You may choose a volunteer to take on the role of Mother – who will then be able to feed back her feelings – what was her 'conscience' telling her to do?

Ask the group to consider the repercussions of Mother's possible actions: what might happen if she tells the police? What could happen if she chooses to protect her son?

In groups of four or five, set learners the task of preparing two short, contrasting scenes, demonstrating the possible outcomes of both decisions.

After sufficient working time, share the pieces, and evaluate their effectiveness. Are the consequences of the mother's decision clear?

Extended learning

As an extension task, individuals are asked to write a letter, in role as Mother, which explains to her son her final decision and her reasons for this.

Workshop 5: Perspectives on the riots

Resources needed for this workshop

Six key statements – lines taken from the play – positioned around the room:

1. 'The walls of the palace came crumbling down …'
2. 'What's happened to the world?'
3. 'A society which does nothing to support the likes of us'.
4. 'A seething mass of foul creatures …'
5. 'They prove that our society is broken'.
6. 'Maybe we need to try and understand?'

Place the six key statements around the room.

Divide the group into six subgroups and ask each group to sit near one statement and discuss their responses to the line.

Now *market place* the statements by asking each group to elect a spokesperson who will move from group to group to share their statement and responses to it. Each spokesperson will move clockwise from group to group when instructed to do so by the teacher. Eventually all statements will have been shared and discussed/ debated.

Groups now decide on one statement which they believe has the most impact and prepare a still image to depict their response to it. After a short amount of time, groups are asked to share their image.

To further develop their work, each group now brings the image to life using strategies of their choice. You may need to discuss strategies first. This will be quite abstract.

After each is shown, the class discuss the impact and meaning of the work.

The final task is for group members to move to one of the statements explored in the lesson and be ready to explain why they felt this statement was the most thought-provoking.

Extended learning

Complete *learner's logs.*

Workshop 6: Unheard voices

> **Resources needed for this workshop**
>
> Images of the UK riots.
>
> Copies or projection of Resource sheet 1.

Show an image of the riots – choose an image where it is clear that there are bystanders who are not directly involved but may have been affected in some way. Ask each group member to choose one person captured in the photograph and consider what that person's thoughts might have been at that particular moment. After some thinking time, ask learners to stand around the edge of the space and walk into the middle to recreate the image as a three-dimensional *whole-class tableau*. If tapped on the shoulder, learners speak the thoughts of their chosen character.

Give some time for reflection:

- How far was your character directly involved in what was going on?
- How did they feel about what was happening?
- What impact did these events have on your character – perhaps some time later?

Explain to the group that they are going to hear the voices of five individuals who were also affected in some way by the riots but may not have been directly involved (see Resource sheet 1).

Resource sheet 1

Person 1: *My dress was burned when that shop was set alight. I never got my money back. It ruined my special day.*

Person 2: *I never did get to that job interview – the tube station was shut.*

Person 3: *I had no way of letting him know that his dad had been admitted to hospital. I just couldn't get hold of him.*

Person 4: *They withdrew the offer on my flat: said it was no place to bring up a child.*

Person 5: *We had to cancel our family holiday. We sat by his bedside until he came round. My little girl was too upset to visit him.*

Riot

Place the learners in groups of five, and give each a copy of Resource sheet 1. Their task is to read the statements and as a group decide who may have said each statement and what they think may have happened, and in particular, what effect the event may have had on the character's life.

After working time allow groups to share their suggestions. Use this exercise to highlight the wider impact of the riots.

Ask each group member to choose one of the five characters (or, for more able students, to create their own), and to write a monologue based on this character's story. This monologue should aim to capture, the description of events, the character's emotion or feelings and perhaps indicate what happened next.

Allow opportunity to share the writing with a learning buddy, so that the work can be developed or improved.

Once a final draft has been completed, allow rehearsal time before the monologues are presented to the whole group. Things for the performers to consider might be:

- Their stage position and use of space.
- Their use of voice gesture and facial expression to convey emotion.
- Their pace of delivery and use of pause to create mood and tension.

Allow time for feedback and reflection on the implications of the work.

Extended learning

Complete *learner's logs*.

PATHWAY 2: KS4 – A PERFORMANCE-SKILLS APPROACH FOR OLDER LEARNERS

Workshop 1: Monologue to dialogue

Resources needed for this workshop

Copies of the play script for *One Summer Evening*.

Paper and pens.

Building blocks

Split the class into eight groups and give each group one monologue to work on. Their task is to highlight any moments described in the monologue which could be adapted into dialogue between two or more characters. Key questions are:

- Who could be involved in the scene?
- Where is it set?
- When does the dialogue take place?
- What is said and why?

Once groups have highlighted these key sections, ask them to begin improvising around one of the highlighted sections. Within each group, learners either take on one of the roles or become directors if there are fewer actors required.

Each group presents to the rest of the class.

The challenge

Learners are now told that the playwright is looking to adapting the monologues into a full play script. Their task is to script the section of dialogue explored in the previous task so that it can now become a scripted scene from the play. It may be necessary here to remind learners of the layout and key components of a script. (Learners may need to be reminded of the conventions of play script notation before they begin this task.)

Top tips/Ask the expert

Each group is paired up with another group and asked to present their scene. The key question for the observers is: Does this scene work, and how could it be developed?

Re-focus and refine

Each group uses the feedback given in the last task to improve their work. After a short amount of time learners are asked to consider the strategy of cross-cutting and another exchange of dialogue/set of characters that they could cut to. They should be given time to experiment with this.

Workshop 2: Creating effective links/transitions between scenes

Resources needed for this workshop

Copies of *One Summer Evening* play script.

Building blocks

Discuss with the class the staging of the monologues. Key questions are:

- How do actors enter/exit the stage?
- How do transitions from one monologue to another happen?

Ask learners to turn to the person next to them to consider these issues. After a short amount of time, ask them to feedback their responses to the rest of the group.

Place learners in groups of four or five and ask them to consider the opening to this piece. Who is on stage? What action takes place before the first monologue is spoken? After five minutes each group presents their introduction. There may need to be an opportunity for evaluative feedback here.

The challenge

Learners now return to their groups and are asked to create the links/transitions which take place between sections. They will need to 'top and tail' each monologue. They could use the opening sequence created in the previous task should they wish to do so.

Top tips/Ask the expert

Groups present the work completed so far to another group in order to receive feedback. Key questions whilst observing are:

- What meanings have been created?
- Does the piece flow?
- Any areas for improvement/development?

Re-focus and refine

Groups now have the opportunity to build on the feedback received in the previous task. You might like to prompt new ideas by highlighting how use of music, multi-media, lighting and symbolism could be incorporated.

Workshop 3: Montage of the night

Resources needed for this workshop

Labelled large sheets of paper and pens

Building blocks

Place large sheets of paper and a pen in four corners of the space. The following is written on each sheet:

Sheet 1: *Characters*

Sheet 2: *Feelings*

Sheet 3: *Events that take place*

Sheet 4: *Settings*

Split the class into four groups and ask each group to sit around one of the four sheets outlined above. They are given five minutes to fill the sheet with ideas relating to whatever title is on their sheet. For example, if the sheet says *settings*, the group have to fill the sheet with all of the settings where the action in each monologue takes place.

After five minutes ask each group to share their responses with the rest of the class so that all ideas can be pooled together.

Now explain the concept of *montage* and how it could be created using the responses from the previous task.

Ask learners to return to the area of the space they were previously working in and to turn over their large sheet of paper. Their next task is to draw their ideas for the creation of a montage of the events of that summer night. This montage on paper will look rather like a collage of illustrations, words and phrases.

After five minutes ask learners to share their responses with the group.

The challenge

Learners are asked to use their ideas from the previous task to create a *montage* of key 'snap shots' of the night with particular focus on soundscape, image, movement, mime and gesture.

Top tips/Ask the expert

Groups are paired up with another group to share their pieces. Key focus questions are:

- How is the *essence* of the night being captured?
- Is the montage effective as drama?
- What improvements could be made?

Re-focus and refine

Groups are now asked to consider if there are any other opportunities in the play when montage could be used. For example, it might be that a montage could be created that depicts one character's perspective, thoughts and feelings. An alternative idea is to create a montage which captures the aftermath of the riots.

Workshop 4: What happens next?

> **Resources needed for this workshop**
>
> A chair!

Building blocks

Learners are asked to take part in a *relay hot-seating* task in order to consolidate their knowledge and understanding of various characters in the piece. Each learner chooses one character from one of the monologues and adopts that character to be *hot-seated*. The idea is that the 'hot seat' should never be left empty and therefore after 30 seconds in the chair, the learner being hot-seated should be replaced quickly by the next.

Learners are now asked what new insight they gained from the previous task. Which characters intrigued them the most?

The challenge

Learners are asked to choose one character explored in the hot-seating task and to consider where their story could go next. Their challenge is to extend the monologue of one of their chosen characters and create a new monologue illustrating what happens subsequently.

Re-focus and refine

Learners pair up with a partner and are given the opportunity to share their new monologue. Observers should be able to feedback their thoughts on whether or not the new monologue 'works' and any improvements that could be made. As an extension task the monologues can be developed into short stories that tell the character's story in more detail.

Workshop 5: Monologues in performance

> **Resources needed for this workshop**
>
> Paper and pens.

Building blocks

Learners take part in a variety of vocal and physical warm-ups at the start of this workshop in order to prepare for the subsequent tasks.

Suggestions might be tongue-twisters, articulating vowel sounds or chewing an imaginary toffee, or playing an active game such as '*Splat!*' or '*Ship Ashore!*'. Learners could also be asked to move around the space experimenting with pace and ways of moving before getting into groups of a given number. Once groups are formed they are asked to complete physical tasks such as creating a prop, object, letter or number by working collaboratively.

The group are now asked to consider what an actor needs to do in order to prepare for a performance of a monologue.

Each learner is asked to write down their own *actor's checklist* before they begin the following task. This should include vocal techniques such as: tone, pace, pitch, volume and use of gesture, movement, facial expression, body language and space. This can be referred to during various points throughout the rest of this workshop.

The challenge

Learners are asked to choose one of the monologues to rehearse and present.

Top tips/Ask the expert

Learners are asked to buddy up with another learner and present their monologue.

Re-focus and refine

In order to re-focus learners and encourage them to think about refining their work you could ask them to take part in the following short exercises:

- Find five key gestures that you could use in your monologue and present to the class.
- Find three different ways of delivering the same line.
- Present your monologue in an underplayed, minimal acting style, a 'normal' style and then in an exaggerated way.
- Present you monologues from three different positions: sitting, standing and from within the audience.
- Consider adding a particular costume or prop.

Now allow time for learners to adapt their work and perhaps alter their *actor's checklist*. They could also add stage directions to their monologues.

Give each learner the opportunity to perform their monologue; as an extension task, ask learners to present the sequence of monologues in a larger group where each member adopts a role. This task offers lots of opportunity to develop independent learning as learners create and experiment with re-sequencing their monologues in various ways.

Things to consider:

- Does re-sequencing the monologues create more impact for an audience? If so, why?
- Does your new sequence provide enough perspective on the events of the riots – how can other character's views be incorporated? Can this be done through 'multi-rolling'?
- What is the most effective stage configuration? Would the piece work better *in the round, end-on,* or with a *promenade* staging?
- Are characters *onstage* all the time? Do they speak directly to the audience, or are the audience 'eavesdropping' on a conversation with an unseen person?

Workshop 6: Exploring the aftermath

Resources needed for this workshop

Copies of the final sequence from the play *One Summer Evening.*

Building blocks

The play ends with a sequence of statements from the various characters caught up in the events of that evening. In groups of nine (to represent each character in the play), learners are asked to stage this ending as scripted. This could be shared with the rest of the group at this stage.

Learners are now asked to consider an alternative ending to the piece. In order to introduce this, ask them to imagine that the repeated line, 'That evening, I. . .' is now, 'One month later, I. . .'

Each group member chooses a character from the piece and, working individually, devises a short continuation from the line, 'One month later, I . . .'

In order to share the work at this stage, tap the individuals on the shoulder to signal their 'spoken thoughts' as the character. Discuss with the group any particularly interesting responses.

The challenge

In groups of four, learners now develop this idea in the form of a scene that is based around two characters, one month later.

Things to consider:

● Which two key characters might be most interesting to explore in the aftermath of the riots? Which pairings might offer the most dramatic potential? Have these characters met before? If so, under what circumstances? If not, what might bring them together?

● How could you present the events that take place for these characters a month after the riots? What links them, or brings them together? Is there contrast in their experiences, attitudes or emotions? What other characters – played by the other group members – might need to be introduced?

● Do the two key characters actually meet? If not, what drama techniques could be employed to present their stories?

Give some working time for groups to devise a rough version of their new scene.

Top tips/Ask the expert

Ask the learners to now focus on their work in progress. In order to do this, ask one group member in each group to 'step out' and become an 'outside eye' able to give direction and suggest adjustments. This role could be alternated to give all members a chance to 'direct'.

Re-focus and refine

Key question for the group at this stage:

- What is the *purpose* of your piece?
- What are you trying to say about the riots, or their impact on the characters involved?

What adjustments now need to be made to ensure that the piece has the desired effect on an audience?

A final task is for the groups to present their 'polished' pieces and allow opportunity for feedback and evaluation. On reflection, what insights do learners feel that they have gained? Are they any clearer about the causes and consequences of the events that took place?

Have their attitudes and opinions altered as they have worked through the unit? If so, how? At what point in the workshops did they feel they gained a different perspective or understanding?